Flavors of India: A Culinary Odyssey in Indian Style : World Cuisines

Prabhakar Veeraraghavan

Published by Prabhakar Veeraraghavan, 2024.

FLAVORS OF INDIA: A CULINARY ODYSSEY IN INDIAN STYLE : WORLD CUISINES

First edition. February 28, 2024.

ISBN: 979-8224544653

Written by Prabhakar Veeraraghavan.

Table of Contents

FLAVORS OF INDIA

A Culinary Odyssey in Indian Style : World Cuisines

Savoring India's Culinery Heritage :
A Feast for the Senses

PRABHAKAR VEERARAGHAVAN

FLAVORS OF INDIA:
A Culinary Odyssey in Indian Style :
World Cuisines

Savouring India's Culinary Heritage:
A Feast for the Senses

By : Prabhakar Veeraraghavan

Copyright © 2024
by Prabhakar Veeraraghavan
All rights reserved.
Type of book

Flavors of India, Culinary Odyssey, World Cuisines, Indian Cuisine, Culinary Exploration, Gastronomic Journey, Indian Flavors, Authentic Recipes, Global Cuisine, Cultural Fusion, Exotic Dishes, Taste of India, International Flavors, Epicurean Adventure, Fusion Cooking

About the author

Prabhakar Veeraraghavan is a seasoned corporate professional turned passionate blogger, KDP author, and seller. With over two decades of experience in the corporate world, Prabhakar has seamlessly transitioned into the world of writing, fuelled by his love for both traveling and cooking. His innate ability to craft captivating words and evoke profound emotions in his readers is evident in every piece of his work.

Beyond merely entertaining his audience, Prabhakar's goal is to immerse them deeply into the subjects he explores, particularly in the realm of cooking. His books not only offer delightful culinary journeys but also aim to benefit readers in various ways. Whether it's discovering new Flavors, mastering cooking techniques, or simply experiencing the joy of creating delicious meals, Prabhakar's writings leave a mind-blowing effect on completion, enriching the lives of his readers in more ways than one.

ALL RIGHTS RESERVED

Disclaimer:

The recipes and information provided in this book are intended for general informational purposes only. While every effort has been made to ensure the accuracy and reliability of the content, the author and publisher make no representations or warranties, express or implied, regarding the completeness, accuracy, reliability, suitability, or availability of the information contained herein.

Readers are advised to use their discretion and judgment when preparing and consuming any dishes based on the recipes provided in this book. It is recommended to follow safe food handling practices, including proper cooking temperatures and storage guidelines, to prevent foodborne illness. The author and publisher shall not be held liable for any loss, damage, or injury resulting from the use of the information contained in this book. Readers are encouraged to consult with a qualified professional, such as a nutritionist or healthcare provider, for specific dietary advice or concerns.

All individuals with food allergies, sensitivities, or dietary restrictions should carefully review the ingredients and preparation methods of each recipe before consuming any dish. It is the responsibility of the reader to verify the suitability of ingredients and make substitutions as necessary to accommodate personal dietary needs. By using this book, readers agree to release the author and publisher from any liability arising from the use or misuse of the information contained herein. Enjoy cooking, exploring, and severing the Flavors of India responsibly and safely.

PRELUDE :

6

A Journey Through Culinary Diversity :

Welcome to "**Flavors of India: A Culinary Odyssey in Indian Style**," where we embark on a journey to Savor the rich and diverse tapestry of Flavors that define Indian cuisine. In this culinary exploration, we invite you to join us as we traverse the vast expanse of this incredible land, from the snow-capped peaks of the Himalayas to the sun-drenched shores of the Indian Ocean.

India, with its 28 states and diverse communities, is a melting pot of cultures, traditions, and culinary delights. Each region boasts its own unique culinary heritage, influenced by geography, climate, history, and cultural practices. From the hearty and robust dishes of the North to the subtle and aromatic Flavors of the South, every corner of India offers a tantalizing array of tastes and aromas waiting to be discovered.

As we journey through the pages of this book, we will delve deep into the heart of Indian cuisine, exploring the vibrant spices, fresh ingredients, and time-honoured cooking techniques that make it so special. From the bustling markets of Mumbai to the serene villages of Kerala, we will get to know about the farmers, artisans, and chefs who bring the Flavors of India to life, sharing their talents and traditions along the way.

But our culinary odyssey is about more than just food – it's about connection, community, and the shared joy of breaking bread together. Whether you're a seasoned chef or a curious home cook, we hope that this book will inspire you to explore the wonders of Indian cuisine in your own kitchen, and to Savor the magic of India's culinary heritage with family and friends.

What's Unique about this book?

Embark on a culinary journey unlike any other with this recipe book. While traditional recipe books typically dive straight into the recipes, this one offers a unique approach. Before delving into the delectable dishes, immerse yourself in the rich tapestry of culinary heritage that defines the essence of the country. Discover the diverse regions, each boasting its own distinct Flavors, ingredients, and cooking techniques. Explore the cultural significance of regional delicacies and uncover the secrets behind their traditional preparation methods. From seasonal delights to festive feasts, this book celebrates the full spectrum of Flavors that grace the table throughout the year. Learn about essential spices and ingredients that lend depth and complexity to every dish, and gain valuable insights into menu planning and meal preparation. But it's not just about the recipes – indulge in captivating culinary stories and anecdotes that offer a glimpse into the soul of the cuisine. So, before you embark on your gastronomic adventure, take a moment to Savor the rich tapestry of Flavors, aromas, and traditions that await within these pages.

So come, join us on this journey of discovery, as we celebrate the vibrant Flavors, rich traditions, and endless possibilities of Indian cooking. Let's embark on a culinary odyssey through the Flavors of India, where every meal is a feast for the senses and a celebration of life itself.

How to use this Recipe Book?

1. **Recipe Overview:** Take a moment to familiarize yourself with the entire recipe before you start cooking. Understanding the overall process will help you plan and gather all the necessary ingredients and tools.

2. **Ingredient Preparation:** Check the ingredients list and ensure you have all the required items ready before you begin cooking. This proactive step will help prevent any missing key ingredients that could affect the final taste of your dish.

3. **Technique Understanding**: Take time to comprehend any specific cooking techniques mentioned in the recipe, such as sautéing, simmering, or braising. Understanding these methods will empower you to execute the recipe with confidence and finesse.

4. **Pre-Cooking Prep**: Before starting to cook, dedicate some time to chop, dice, and prepare all the ingredients as instructed in the recipe. This preparatory work will streamline the cooking process and ensure smooth execution.

5. **Measurement Precision**: Pay careful attention to measurements and proportions as indicated in the recipe. Accuracy in measuring ingredients is crucial for achieving the desired flavour and texture in your dish.

6. **Taste Testing**: Don't hesitate to taste your dish as you progress through the cooking process. Sampling along the way allows you to adjust seasoning and fine-tune the Flavors to your liking.

7.**Creative Exploration**: Embrace creativity and experiment with suggested accompaniments or variations to personalize the dish. Cooking is an art, so feel free to add your unique touch to each recipe.

8. **Success Strategies**: Utilize quality ingredients, balance Flavors, and maintain proper temperature control throughout cooking to optimize your chances of achieving the best possible outcome.

9. **Practiced Patience**: Recognize that cooking requires patience and attention to detail. Approach each step with care and take pleasure in the journey, knowing that the end result will be rewarding.

10.**Aesthetic Presentation**: Elevate the dining experience by paying attention to the presentation of your dishes. A visually appealing meal enhances enjoyment and creates a memorable dining experience.

11.**Take Pictures and Share Enjoyment:** Share your culinary creations with loved ones and relish the joy of communal dining. Food has a unique ability to bring people together and create cherished memories.

12. **Learning from Experience:** Embrace mistakes as learning opportunities and strive to glean insights from every cooking endeavour. Each experience contributes to your growth and refinement as a cook.

Introduction : Flavors of India: A Culinary Odyssey

A Culinary Odyssey:

Welcome to the enchanting world of Indian cuisine, where every dish tells a story and every flavour evokes a symphony of senses. India, a land of vibrant colours, rich in traditions, and diverse cultures, boasts a culinary heritage as varied and complex as its landscape. From the majestic peaks of the Himalayas to the sun-kissed shores of the Indian Ocean, each region of this vast and diverse country offers its own unique Flavors, ingredients, and cooking techniques, reflecting centuries of history, trade, and cultural exchange.

Step into any kitchen in India, and you'll be greeted with the intoxicating aromas of spices sizzling in hot oil, the rhythmic sounds of grinding masalas, and the warmth of hospitality that permeates every meal. Food isn't just sustenance in India; it's a celebration of life, a reflection of love and affection, and a bridge that connects people across boundaries of language, religion, and caste.

India, as the world leader in spices, showcases a profound reverence for nature, its abundant offerings and the bountiful gifts it provides at the heart of Indian cuisine. From the humble lentil and rice to the exotic spices like cardamom, cloves, and cinnamon, Indian cooking celebrates the abundance of the land, elevating simple ingredients into culinary masterpieces that delight the senses and nourish the soul.

But Indian cuisine isn't just about the food; it's also about the customs, rituals, and traditions that accompany every meal. In India, cooking is an art form passed down through generations, with recipes handed down from mother to daughter, father to son, and shared among friends and neighbours in a spirit of camaraderie and community.

From the elaborate feasts of festivals like Diwali, Eid, and Christmas to the simple pleasures of a home-cooked meal shared with loved ones, food plays a central role in every aspect of Indian life. It's a way of expressing love and gratitude, of honouring guests and welcoming strangers, and of connecting with our cultural roots and heritage.

In this cookbook, we invite you to embark on a culinary journey through the diverse Flavors and traditions of India. From the fiery curries of the North to the delicate seafood dishes of the South, each recipe is a testament to the rich tapestry of Flavors and influences that make Indian cuisine so unique.

So, join us as we explore the sights, sounds, and tastes of India – from the bustling markets of Mumbai to the serene backwaters of Kerala – and discover the magic of Indian cooking for yourself. Whether you're a seasoned chef or a novice cook, there's something here for everyone to Savor, enjoy, and celebrate. Welcome to the Flavors of India – where every meal is a feast for the senses and a journey of discovery.

The Essence of Indian Cuisine:

"The Essence of Indian Cuisine" delves into the fundamental aspects that define and distinguish Indian culinary traditions. At its core, Indian cuisine embodies a rich tapestry of Flavors, textures, aromas, and colours that reflect the country's diverse cultural heritage, geography, and history.

Flavour Palette: Indian cuisine is renowned for its bold and complex flavour profiles, which are achieved through the skilful blending of aromatic spices, herbs, and seasonings. From the fiery heat of chili peppers to the subtle sweetness of cardamom and the earthy richness of cumin, each spice contributes to a symphony of tastes that tantalize the taste buds.

Regional Diversity: One of the most remarkable aspects of Indian cuisine is its vast regional diversity, with each region boasting its own distinctive culinary traditions, ingredients, and techniques. From the hearty meat-based dishes of the North to the vegetarian delicacies of the South and the seafood specialties of the coastal regions, Indian cuisine offers a plethora of Flavors and textures to explore.

Vegetarian Emphasis: A significant aspect of Indian cuisine is its emphasis on vegetarianism, which has deep cultural, religious, and philosophical roots. Vegetarian dishes are celebrated for their creativity, variety, and nutritional balance, showcasing an array of vegetables, legumes, grains, and dairy products prepared in innovative and delicious ways.

Balance of Tastes: Central to Indian cooking is the concept of balancing the six tastes – sweet, sour, salty, bitter, pungent, and astringent – in every meal to create harmony and satisfaction. This balance is achieved through the careful selection and combination of ingredients, as well as the use of techniques such as tempering, marinating, and simmering.

Cultural Significance: Indian cuisine is deeply intertwined with the country's cultural heritage, traditions, and rituals, playing a central role in social gatherings, festivals, and religious ceremonies. Food is not just nourishment; it is a form of expression, a means of fostering community, and a way of preserving cultural identity.

Adaptability and Innovation: Despite its rich culinary traditions, Indian cuisine is also marked by its adaptability and innovation, with chefs and home cooks constantly experimenting with new ingredients, techniques, and flavour combinations. This spirit of creativity and evolution ensures that Indian cuisine remains vibrant, dynamic, and relevant in an ever-changing world.

In essence, Indian cuisine is a celebration of diversity, creativity, and tradition, offering a feast for the senses and a glimpse into the rich tapestry of Indian culture and heritage. Whether enjoyed at home, in a street-side eatery, or at a lavish banquet, Indian food never fails to captivate, inspire, and delight.

The Diversity of Indian Flavors

"The Diversity of Indian Flavors" celebrates the kaleidoscope of tastes and aromas that define Indian cuisine, showcasing the remarkable variety of ingredients, spices, and culinary traditions found across the subcontinent.

Regional Variation: Indian cuisine is renowned for its regional diversity, with each state and region boasting its own unique culinary traditions, ingredients, and Flavors. From the fiery curries of the North to the coconut-infused dishes of the South and the aromatic biryanis of the East, the culinary landscape of India is as vast and varied as its geography.

Cultural Influence: The diversity of Indian Flavors is a testament to the country's rich cultural heritage and history of trade and migration. Over the centuries, Indian cuisine has been shaped by the influences of various cultures, including Persian, Mughal, Portuguese, and British, resulting in a fusion of Flavors and ingredients that is truly unparalleled.

Spice Blends: At the heart of Indian cooking are the iconic spice blends, or masalas, which lend depth, complexity, and character to dishes. From the fragrant garam masala of the North to the tangy sambar powder of the South and the fiery vindaloo masala of Goa, each spice blend has its own unique combination of spices and herbs, resulting in a myriad of Flavors and aromas.

Vegetarian Delicacies: Indian cuisine is renowned for its vegetarian offerings, which showcase the versatility and creativity of plant-based cooking. From the hearty lentil stews of Punjab to the crispy dosas of South India and the comforting khichdi of Gujarat, vegetarian dishes are celebrated for their rich flavors and nutritional value.

Seafood and Meat: While vegetarianism plays a significant role in Indian cuisine, seafood and meat dishes are also integral to many regional cuisines. From the succulent kebabs of Lucknow to the spicy fish curries of Kerala and the aromatic biryanis of Hyderabad, Indian cuisine offers a wide range of options for seafood and meat lovers alike.

Street Food Culture: Indian street food is a vibrant and essential aspect of the country's culinary landscape, offering a tantalizing array of Flavors and textures that reflect the diversity of Indian cuisine. From the Savory chaats of Delhi to the spicy vada pavs of Mumbai and the sweet jalebis of Kolkata, street food vendors across India serve up an eclectic mix of snacks and treats that are beloved by locals and visitors alike.

In conclusion, the diversity of Indian Flavors is a testament to the country's rich culinary heritage, cultural diversity, and spirit of innovation. From the bold spices and vibrant colours of North Indian cuisine to the subtle aromas and delicate Flavors of South Indian cooking, Indian cuisine offers a culinary journey like no other, inviting food lovers to explore, Savor, and celebrate the myriad tastes of India.

Regional Delicacies: A Culinary Tour of India

North Indian Cuisine:

Mughlai: Rich, creamy dishes influenced by Mughal cooking, known for dishes like Biryani, Kebabs, and Korma.

Punjabi: Flavourful dishes characterized by robust spices and dairy, including dishes like Butter Chicken, Sarson da Saag, and Makki di Roti.

Kashmiri: Unique dishes featuring saffron, dry fruits, and mild spices, such as Rogan Josh and Yakini.

Awadhi: Royal cuisine from Lucknow, known for slow-cooked dishes like Dum Biriyani and Galouti Kebabs.

South Indian Cuisine:

Tamil Nadu: Spicy and aromatic dishes featuring rice, lentils, and coconut, including Dosa, Idli, and Sambar.

Kerala: Coastal cuisine known for its use of coconut, curry leaves, and seafood, with dishes like Appam, Fish Curry, and Avial.

Andhra Pradesh: Spicy and tangy dishes featuring chili peppers and tamarind, such as Hyderabadi Biryani and Gongura Chicken.

Karnataka: Diverse cuisine with influences from coastal, North Indian, and Udupi traditions, including Bisi Bele Bath, Rava Idli, and Mysore Pak.

East Indian Cuisine:

Bengali: Flavourful dishes with mustard oil, fish, and Bengali five-spice blend (panch phoron), like Machher Jhol, Chingri Macher Malai Curry, and Mishti Doi.

Odia: Simple yet flavourful cuisine featuring rice, lentils, and seafood, including Dalma, Chenna Poda, and Pakhala Bhata.

Assamese: Light and nutritious dishes with rice, fish, and greens, such as Masor Tenga, Khar, and Assamese Thali.

West Indian Cuisine:

Gujarati: Vegetarian cuisine with sweet, spicy, and tangy flavors, including Dhokla, Undhiyu, and Gujarati Kadhi.

Maharashtrian: Varied cuisine with dishes like Vada Pav, Pav Bhaji, and Puran Poli, reflecting both coastal and inland influences.

Goan: Influenced by Portuguese colonialism, known for spicy seafood dishes like Goan Fish Curry, Vindaloo, and Xacuti.

Central Indian Cuisine:

Madhya Pradesh: Diverse cuisine with influences from neighboring regions, featuring dishes like Poha, Bhutte Ka Kees, and Dal Bafla.

Chhattisgarh: Traditional tribal cuisine with dishes like Chousela, Farra, and Bhajia.

Street Food:

Chaat: Savory snacks like Pani Puri, Bhel Puri, and Aloo Tikki Chaat.

Vada Pav: Spicy potato fritter sandwich from Mumbai.

Samosa: Deep-fried pastry filled with spiced potatoes or meat.

Kebabs: Grilled skewered meats like Seekh Kebab and Chicken Tikka.

Dabeli: Spicy potato sandwich with sweet and tangy chutneys.

Jhal Muri: Spicy puffed rice snack from West Bengal.

These are just a few examples of the diverse varieties of Indian cuisine, each with its own unique Flavors, ingredients, and cooking techniques.

Indian Customs, Foods, and Lifestyles

India is a mosaic of cultures, each with its own customs, foods, and lifestyles that shape the everyday lives of its people. From the snow-capped peaks of the Himalayas to the tropical beaches of the south, every region boasts a distinct way of life that is reflected in its culinary traditions.

North India:

In the northern regions of India, customs and foods are deeply intertwined with the changing seasons. Winter brings hearty dishes like sarson da saag and makki di roti, while summer sees the emergence of cooling treats like lassi and aam panna. The tradition of offering "pranam" or "namaskaram" to elders is deeply ingrained in North Indian culture, reflecting the values of respect and humility.

South India:

South Indian customs are characterized by a reverence for tradition and spirituality. Meals are often served on banana leaves, a practice rooted in ancient customs and beliefs. Temples play a central role in South Indian life, with festivals and rituals offering opportunities for communal worship and celebration. From the intricate kolams adorning doorsteps to the rhythmic beats of classical music, South Indian lifestyles are steeped in art and culture.

East India:

In the eastern states of India, customs and foods are influenced by the region's rich history and cultural diversity. Fish forms an integral part of the diet, with dishes like maach bhaja and ilish maach paturi showcasing the culinary prowess of the region. Festivals like Durga Puja and Rath Yatra are celebrated with grand processions and elaborate feasts, bringing communities together in joyous revelry.

West India:

The western states of India are known for their vibrant festivals and colourful customs. From the dandiya raas of Gujarat to the Ganesh Chaturthi celebrations of Maharashtra, every occasion is marked by music, dance, and feasting. The tradition of eating together as a family, known as "ghar ka khana," is cherished in West Indian households, fostering a sense of unity and togetherness.

Central India:

Central India is a land of contrasts, where ancient customs coexist with modern influences. The tradition of hospitality is paramount, with guests often welcomed with open arms and lavish spreads. Traditional dishes like poha and bafla bati reflect the region's agrarian roots, while festivals like Diwali and Navratri offer opportunities for spiritual reflection and community bonding.

Indian customs, foods, and lifestyles are as diverse and dynamic as the country itself, offering a glimpse into the rich tapestry of Indian culture. Whether it's the seasonal delicacies of North India or the temple rituals of South India, every tradition is a reflection of the values, beliefs, and heritage of its people. As we explore the customs and lifestyles of India, let us celebrate the beauty and diversity of this incredible land.

Cooking Techniques and Tips

"Cooking Techniques and Tips" offers a comprehensive exploration of the essential methods and practices that form the foundation of Indian culinary mastery. From the art of tempering spices to the intricacies of dough-making, this section provides invaluable insights and guidance to help both novice and seasoned cooks elevate their cooking skills to new heights.

Tempering (Tadka): Central to Indian cooking is the technique of tempering, or tadka, which involves frying whole spices in hot oil or ghee to release their Flavors and aromas. Whether its cumin seeds sizzling in mustard oil for a North Indian dal or mustard seeds crackling in coconut oil for a South Indian curry, mastering the art of tempering is essential for adding depth and complexity to dishes.

Spice Blending: Indian cuisine is renowned for its intricate spice blends, known as masalas, which are the building blocks of flavour in many dishes. From the aromatic garam masala of North India to the tangy Rasam powder of South India, understanding how to blend and balance spices is key to achieving authentic and delicious results.

Marination: Marinating meat, seafood, or vegetables in a mixture of yogurt, spices, and herbs is a common technique in Indian cooking, imparting flavour, tenderness, and moisture to the ingredients. Whether it's marinating chicken for tandoori or paneer for tikka, allowing sufficient time for marination enhances the taste and texture of the final dish.

Slow Cooking: Many traditional Indian dishes benefit from slow cooking over low heat, allowing the Flavors to develop and meld together over time. Whether it's simmering a pot of dal for hours on the stovetop or cooking a biryani in a sealed pot over a slow flame, patience is rewarded with dishes that are rich, aromatic, and deeply satisfying.

Dough Preparation: From the soft and pillowy naan bread to the crispy and flaky parathas, mastering the art of dough preparation is essential for creating authentic Indian breads. Whether it's kneading the dough to the right consistency or rolling it out evenly, attention to detail is key to achieving perfect results.

Layering Flavors: Indian cooking often involves layering Flavors at various stages of the cooking process to build complexity and depth. Whether it's caramelizing onions to add sweetness to a curry or adding a splash of lime juice at the end to brighten the Flavors, understanding how to layer Flavors enhances the overall taste and balance of a dish.

Balancing Heat: Indian cuisine is known for its bold and spicy Flavors, but achieving the right balance of heat is essential for a well-rounded dish. Whether it's adjusting the amount of chili powder in a curry or adding a dollop of yogurt to cool the palate, knowing how to balance heat ensures that every bite is flavourful and enjoyable.

Tandoori Cooking:

Tandoori roti is a traditional Indian flatbread that is loved for its smoky flavour and fluffy texture. Making tandoori roti involves a unique cooking technique where the dough is slapped onto the walls of a tandoor, a clay oven heated by charcoal or wood fire. The intense heat of the tandoor cooks the roti quickly, resulting in a slightly charred exterior and soft interior. To prepare the dough, a mixture of whole wheat flour, water, and salt is kneaded until it forms a smooth and elastic dough. Small portions of the dough are then rolled into round discs and cooked in the tandoor until they puff up and develop a golden brown colour. The end result is a delicious and aromatic bread that pairs perfectly with a variety of Indian dishes.

Garnishing and Presentation: The final touch to any Indian dish is the garnish, which adds visual appeal and enhances the overall presentation. Whether it's sprinkling fresh cilantro over a curry or drizzling a swirl of cream over a dessert, attention to detail in garnishing elevates the dining experience and delights the senses.

Following are some more common cooking techniques used by Home Chefs and Stret food makers

Sauteing

Sauteing involves cooking food quickly in a small amount of oil or fat over medium to high heat. This technique is commonly used for vegetables, meats, and aromatics like onions and garlic to develop flavour and texture.

Grilling

Grilling involves cooking food over direct heat on a grill or barbecue. It imparts a smoky flavour and caramelization to meats, vegetables, and seafood, making it a popular outdoor cooking method.

Roasting

Roasting involves cooking food in an oven at high temperatures, typically above 400°F (200°C). It is used for meats, vegetables, and even fruits, resulting in caramelization and intense Flavors.

Steaming

Steaming involves cooking food by exposing it to steam from boiling water. It is a gentle and healthy cooking method that retains the natural Flavors, colours, and nutrients of the ingredients.

Boiling

Boiling involves cooking food in boiling water at 100°C (212°F). It is used for pasta, grains, vegetables, and eggs, and can be adjusted to achieve different levels of doneness.

Stir-Frying

Stir-frying involves cooking food quickly in a wok or frying pan over high heat with constant stirring. It is a versatile technique used in Asian cuisine for vegetables, meats, and noodles.

Braising

Braising involves cooking food slowly in a flavourful liquid, such as broth or wine, at low temperatures. It is used for tougher cuts of meat and root vegetables to tenderize and infuse them with flavour.

Baking

Baking involves cooking food in an oven using dry heat. It is used for bread, cakes, cookies, and pastries, resulting in a crisp exterior and tender interior.

Seasoning

Seasoning involves adding salt, pepper, herbs, spices, and other flavorings to enhance the taste of food. It is important to taste and adjust seasoning throughout the cooking process to achieve a balanced flavour profile.

Knife Skills

Good knife skills are essential for efficient and safe cooking. Learning proper cutting techniques, such as chopping, dicing, mincing, and slicing, can improve the appearance and texture of dishes.

Temperature Control

Proper temperature control is crucial for achieving optimal cooking results. Understanding the appropriate cooking temperatures for different ingredients and adjusting heat sources accordingly can prevent overcooking or undercooking.

Mastering the essential cooking techniques and tips of Indian cuisine is the key to creating delicious, authentic, and memorable dishes. Whether you're a novice cook or an experienced chef, understanding these fundamentals will empower you to explore the rich and diverse world of Indian cooking with confidence and creativity.

Organization and Preparation

Organizing and preparing ingredients before cooking, can streamline the cooking process and ensure that everything is ready when needed. This includes chopping vegetables, measuring ingredients, and preheating equipment.

Experimentation and Adaptation

Don't be afraid to experiment with Flavors, ingredients, and techniques in the kitchen. Cooking is a creative process, and adapting recipes to suit your taste preferences and dietary needs can lead to delicious and personalized dishes.

Deglazing

Deglazing involves adding liquid (such as wine, broth, or vinegar) to a hot pan to loosen and dissolve the flavourful browned bits (fond) that are stuck to the bottom after searing meat or sautéing vegetables. This technique adds depth and richness to sauces and gravies.

Simmering

Simmering is a gentle cooking technique where food is cooked in liquid at a temperature just below boiling point, typically around 180°F to 200°F (80°C to 93°C). It is used to cook soups, stews, sauces, and braises slowly and evenly, allowing Flavors to meld and develop over time.

Blanching

Blanching involves briefly immersing food in boiling water, then quickly transferring it to ice-cold water to stop the cooking process. This technique is used to soften vegetables, remove skins from fruits or nuts, and brighten the colour of green vegetables before freezing or further cooking.

Poaching

Poaching involves gently cooking food in liquid at low temperatures, usually between 160°F to 180°F (71°C to 82°C). It is commonly used for delicate foods like eggs, fish, chicken, and fruits, resulting in tender and moist textures.

Whisking and Emulsifying

Whisking involves vigorously beating ingredients together to incorporate air and create a smooth and uniform mixture. Emulsifying is a process of combining two liquids that are usually unmixable, such as oil and vinegar, to form a stable mixture, like vinaigrettes and mayonnaise.

Resting and Tenting

Resting refers to allowing cooked meat to sit undisturbed for a few minutes before slicing or serving. This allows the juices to redistribute throughout the meat, resulting in juicier and more flavourful slices. Tenting involves covering the meat loosely with foil to keep it warm while resting.

These cooking techniques and tips expand your culinary repertoire and help you achieve better results in the kitchen. Whether you're a novice cook or an experienced chef, mastering these techniques will enhance your cooking skills and make your dishes even more delicious.

By mastering these cooking techniques and tips, home cooks can elevate their culinary skills, expand their repertoire of recipes, and create delicious and satisfying meals for themselves and their loved ones.

Essential Spices and Ingredients

The secrets of any tasty dish are the ingredients and rarely any Chef reveals about the secret ingredients, present in the dish. This section provides an overview of essential spices, herbs, and other ingredients commonly used in Indian cooking that makes the dish taste out of the world. With the names of the ingredients and their speciality, these spices can be used in the dish to make them a mouthwatering one.

Turmeric (Haldi):

Known for its vibrant yellow colour, turmeric is a staple spice in Indian cuisine. It adds colour and earthy flavour to dishes and is also valued for its medicinal properties.

Cumin (Jeera):

Cumin seeds are widely used for tempering (tadka) in Indian dishes. They impart a warm, nutty flavour and aroma to curries, rice dishes, and lentil preparations.

Coriander (Dhania):

Coriander seeds and ground coriander powder are essential spices in Indian cooking. They add a citrusy, floral flavour to dishes and are commonly used in curries, chutneys, and marinades.

Cinnamon (Dalchini):

Cinnamon sticks or ground cinnamon are used to impart a warm and sweet flavour to Indian dishes. They are often added to rice dishes, desserts, and meat curries.

Cardamom (Elaichi):

Both green and black cardamom pods are used in Indian cuisine. They add a floral and slightly spicy flavour to dishes and are often used in rice preparations, desserts, and masala chai.

Cloves (Laung):

Cloves are known for their strong and pungent flavor. They are used whole or ground in spice blends, rice dishes, meat curries, and marinades.

Black Mustard Seeds (Rai):

Black mustard seeds are commonly used for tempering in Indian cooking. They add a nutty and slightly bitter flavour to dishes and are often used in pickles, curries, and stir-fries.

Fenugreek (Methi):

Fenugreek seeds and fenugreek leaves (kasuri methi) are used in Indian cooking. Fenugreek seeds have a slightly bitter taste and are used in spice blends and pickles, while fenugreek leaves are used to flavour curries and lentil dishes.

Garam Masala:

Garam masala is a blend of ground spices commonly used in Indian cooking. It typically includes spices like cloves, cardamom, cinnamon, cumin, and coriander, adding warmth and complexity to dishes.

Ginger and Garlic:

Fresh ginger and garlic are essential ingredients in Indian cooking. They add aromatic flavour and depth to dishes and are often used in marinades, curries, and stir-fries.

Chili Powder (Lal Mirch):

Chili powder adds heat and colour to Indian dishes. It can be made from various types of dried chili peppers and is used to spice up curries, marinades, and snacks.

Curry Leaves:

Curry leaves are used for tempering and flavouring in South Indian cuisine. They add a distinctive aroma and flavour to dishes like curries, rice preparations, and chutneys.

Asafoetida (Hing):

Asafoetida is a pungent and aromatic spice used in Indian cooking, especially in vegetarian dishes. It enhances the flavour of lentils, beans, and vegetables and aids in digestion.

Fennel Seeds (Saunf):

Fennel seeds have a sweet and licorice-like flavour and are commonly used as a digestive aid in Indian cuisine. They are also used to flavour meat dishes, pickles, and desserts.

Nigella Seeds (Kalonji):

Nigella seeds, also known as black cumin or kalonji, have a slightly bitter and peppery flavour. They are often used in spice blends, pickles, bread, and vegetable dishes.

Ajwain (Carom Seeds):

Ajwain seeds have a strong and pungent flavour with thyme-like undertones. They are commonly used in bread, lentil dishes, and fried snacks for their digestive properties.

Amchur (Dried Mango Powder):

Amchur adds a tangy and sour flavour to dishes without adding moisture. It is made from dried unripe mangoes and is commonly used in curries, chutneys, and marinades.

Kokum:

Kokum is a dried fruit with a sour taste commonly used in coastal Indian cuisine. It adds a tangy flavour to curries, soups, and drinks and is also used as a natural souring agent.

Poppy Seeds (Khus Khus):

Poppy seeds have a nutty flavour and are often used as a thickening agent in Indian curries and gravies. They are also used to add texture and flavour to bread, pastries, and desserts.

Saffron (Kesar):

Saffron is a prized spice known for its vibrant colour and floral aroma. It is used to flavour and colour dishes like biryanis, desserts, and milk-based beverages.

Star Anise:

Star anise has a strong and licorice-like flavour and is commonly used in spice blends, marinades, and meat dishes. It adds depth and complexity to curries and stews.

Tamarind (Imli):

Tamarind pulp adds a tangy and sour flavour to dishes and is commonly used in South Indian and Maharashtrian cuisine. It is used to make chutneys, sauces, and tangy rice dishes.

Black Salt (Kala Namak):

Black salt, also known as kala namak, has a distinctive sulphurous flavour and is commonly used in chaats, chutneys, and Savory snacks for its tangy taste.

Curry Powder:

Curry powder is a blend of various spices like coriander, cumin, turmeric, and fenugreek, commonly used in Indian cooking to impart flavour and colour to dishes like curries, stews, and marinades.

Jaggery (Gur):

Jaggery is a traditional sweetener made from sugarcane juice or palm sap. It adds a unique sweetness and depth of flavour to Indian desserts, sweets, and Savory dishes.

These spices and ingredients further enrich the depth and complexity of Indian cuisine, allowing for a wide range of Flavors and culinary experiences.

These essential spices and ingredients further enrich the depth and complexity of Indian cuisine, allowing cooks to create a wide range of flavourful and aromatic dishes that are enjoyed by people around the world.

Traditional vs. Modern Indian Food

Indian cuisine is a mix of traditional Indian recipes and modern adaptations of classical dishes, passed down through generations. This can appeal to both those looking for authentic recipes and those interested in innovative twists.

Differentiating between traditional and modern Indian food in your cookbook offers readers a glimpse into the evolving culinary landscape of India. Here's an elaboration along with some dish names for each category:

Traditional Indian Food:

Traditional Indian food refers to dishes that have been passed down through generations, often deeply rooted in cultural and regional traditions. These dishes typically use age-old recipes, cooking techniques, and locally sourced ingredients.

Biryani: A classic traditional dish that originated in Mughlai cuisine, featuring fragrant rice cooked with meat (such as chicken, mutton, or beef) and a blend of aromatic spices.

Malabar Parota: Originating from the Malabar region of Kerala, India. It is a popular flatbread made from refined flour, ghee (clarified butter)

Paneer Tikka: Cubes of paneer (Indian cottage cheese as you call Tofu elsewhere). However Paneer is made from milk and Tofu is made from soya. Marinated in a mixture of yogurt and spices, skewered and grilled to perfection.

Samosa: Triangular pastry filled with a spicy mixture of potatoes, peas, and spices, deep-fried until golden brown and crispy.

Rajma Chawal: A comforting North Indian dish consisting of red kidney beans cooked in a thick tomato-based gravy, served with steamed rice.

Masoor Dal: Simple yet flavourful lentil dish made with red lentils, tempered with onions, tomatoes, and aromatic spices.

Dhokla: Steamed Savory cake made from fermented rice and chickpea flour batter, typically served as a snack or breakfast item in Gujarat.

Modern Indian Food

Modern Indian food represents a fusion of traditional Indian Flavors and cooking techniques with contemporary culinary trends and global influences. These dishes often feature creative interpretations, innovative presentations, and experimental combinations of ingredients.

Butter Chicken Pizza: A modern twist on traditional butter chicken, featuring marinated chicken tikka pieces, creamy tomato sauce, and mozzarella cheese on a pizza crust.

Quinoa Upma: A healthier alternative to traditional semolina-based upma, made with quinoa, vegetables, and spices, offering a nutritious and gluten-free breakfast option.

Paneer Tikka Tacos: A fusion of Indian and Mexican cuisines, featuring grilled paneer tikka served in soft corn tortillas with fresh salsa, guacamole, and a drizzle of mint yogurt sauce.

Vegan Mango Lassi Smoothie Bowl: A contemporary take on the classic Indian yogurt-based drink, mango lassi, served as a thick smoothie bowl topped with granola, fresh fruit, and coconut flakes.

Turmeric Latte: A trendy beverage inspired by traditional Indian haldi doodh (turmeric milk), featuring steamed milk infused with turmeric, ginger, cinnamon, and a hint of sweetness, enjoyed as a soothing and healthful drink.

Avocado Chaat: A modern twist on the beloved Indian street food, chaat, featuring diced avocado tossed with tangy tamarind chutney, mint-coriander chutney, crunchy sev, and chaat masala, offering a refreshing and nutritious appetizer option.

By including a mix of traditional and modern Indian food in your cookbook, you'll cater to a wide range of tastes and preferences, appealing to both purists who seek authentic Flavors and adventurous food enthusiasts who crave innovation and experimentation.

Seasonal Recipes:

In Seasonal recipes we will focus on utilizing ingredients that are in season during specific times of the year.

Spring Recipes:

Spring brings a bounty of fresh vegetables and fruits, signalling the beginning of lighter, fresher dishes after the heaviness of winter. Spring recipes often feature vibrant colours and Flavors.

Green Pea Soup: A light and refreshing soup made with fresh green peas, flavoured with mint and lemon zest.

Asparagus Salad: A crisp salad featuring tender asparagus spears, mixed greens, cherry tomatoes, and a tangy vinaigrette.

Strawberry Spinach Salad: A delightful combination of fresh spinach leaves, juicy strawberries, sliced almonds, and feta cheese, tossed in a balsamic dressing.

Herb-Roasted Spring Vegetables: A medley of spring vegetables such as baby carrots, new potatoes, and baby artichokes, tossed with olive oil and fresh herbs, then roasted until tender.

Lemon Herb Grilled Chicken: Succulent chicken breasts marinated in a mixture of lemon juice, garlic, and fresh herbs, then grilled to perfection.

Rhubarb Crisp: A classic spring dessert featuring tart rhubarb topped with a sweet and crunchy oat crumble, served warm with vanilla ice cream.

Summer Recipes:

Summer brings an abundance of ripe fruits, colourful vegetables, and warm weather, inspiring light and refreshing dishes that are perfect for outdoor dining and picnics.

Caprese Salad: A classic Italian salad made with ripe tomatoes, fresh mozzarella cheese, basil leaves, drizzled with balsamic glaze and olive oil.

Watermelon Feta Salad: A refreshing salad featuring juicy watermelon cubes, crumbled feta cheese, mint leaves, and a splash of lime juice.

Grilled Corn on the Cob: Sweet corn brushed with garlic butter and grilled until charred, then sprinkled with chili powder and fresh cilantro.

Mango Salsa: A tropical salsa made with ripe mangoes, diced red onions, jalapeños, cilantro, and lime juice, perfect for topping grilled fish or chicken.

Peach Caprese Skewers: Skewers of ripe peaches, fresh mozzarella balls, and basil leaves, drizzled with honey and balsamic reduction.

Berry Cobbler: A summer dessert featuring a mix of fresh berries topped with a buttery biscuit crust, baked until golden brown and bubbly.

Autumn Recipes:

Autumn brings cooler temperatures and a harvest of hearty vegetables, root crops, and fall fruits, inspiring cozy and comforting dishes that are perfect for warming up.

Butternut Squash Soup: A creamy and velvety soup made with roasted butternut squash, onions, garlic, and warm spices like cinnamon and nutmeg.

Apple Walnut Salad: A crunchy salad featuring mixed greens, sliced apples, toasted walnuts, crumbled blue cheese, and a maple vinaigrette dressing.

Pumpkin Risotto: Creamy risotto made with Arborio rice, pumpkin puree, Parmesan cheese, and a hint of sage, topped with crispy fried sage leaves.

Roasted Brussels Sprouts: Brussels sprouts tossed with olive oil, balsamic vinegar, and honey, then roasted until caramelized and crispy.

Chicken and Mushroom Stew: A hearty stew made with tender chicken, earthy mushrooms, carrots, celery, onions, and thyme, simmered in a flavourful broth.

Pear Galette: A rustic tart made with thinly sliced pears, sprinkled with sugar and cinnamon, then wrapped in a flaky pastry crust and baked until golden brown.

Winter Recipes:

Winter recipes focus on hearty, warming dishes that provide comfort and nourishment during the colder months. These recipes often feature rich Flavors and ingredients that are in season during the winter.

Beef and Vegetable Stew: A comforting stew made with tender beef, root vegetables like carrots and potatoes, onions, and aromatic herbs, simmered in a rich beef broth.

Creamy Potato Leek Soup: A velvety soup made with potatoes, leeks, onions, garlic, and thyme, blended until smooth and creamy.

Roasted Root Vegetables: A medley of winter root vegetables such as carrots, parsnips, turnips, and rutabagas, tossed with olive oil and roasted until caramelized and tender.

Baked Acorn Squash: Acorn squash halves filled with a Savory mixture of quinoa, mushrooms, spinach, and Parmesan cheese, baked until the squash is tender and the filling is golden brown.

Chicken Pot Pie: A classic comfort food dish featuring tender chicken, mixed vegetables, and a creamy sauce, topped with a flaky pastry crust and baked until golden brown.

Chocolate Peppermint Bark: A festive dessert made with layers of dark and white chocolate, sprinkled with crushed peppermint candies, and chilled until set, then broken into pieces.

By including seasonal recipes in your cookbook, you'll help readers make the most of fresh, seasonal ingredients while celebrating the Flavors and traditions of each season.

Festive and Celebration Foods

Highlight recipes that are traditionally prepared during Indian festivals and celebrations, such as Diwali, Holi, Eid, Navratri, and Christmas. Include sweets, snacks, and main dishes specific to each occasion.

Certainly! Festive and celebration foods are an integral part of Indian culture, often prepared during special occasions, festivals, and ceremonies. These dishes are rich in flavour, symbolism, and tradition, reflecting the spirit of joy and togetherness. Here's an elaboration along with some dish names for festive and celebration foods:

Diwali:

Diwali, also known as the Festival of Lights, is one of the most celebrated festivals in India. It symbolizes the victory of light over darkness and good over evil. Traditional sweets and Savory snacks are prepared and shared with loved ones during Diwali.

Sohan Papdi: A delicate and flaky sweet made from caramelized sugar, ghee, and flour, often flavoured with cardamom and topped with almonds or pistachios.

Kaju Katli: A classic Indian sweet made from ground cashews, sugar, and ghee, shaped into diamond-shaped pieces and garnished with silver leaf.

Chakli: Crispy spiral-shaped snacks made from rice flour, urad dal flour, and spices, deep-fried until golden brown, a popular Savory snack during Diwali.

Gulab Jamun: Soft and spongy milk-based dumplings soaked in sugar syrup, flavoured with rose water and cardamom, a beloved dessert enjoyed during Diwali celebrations.

Holi:

Holi, also known as the Festival of Colours, is a vibrant and joyous celebration that marks the arrival of spring. It is characterized by playful water fights and the throwing of coloured powders. Traditional sweets and snacks are prepared and shared during Holi festivities.

Gujiya: Deep-fried dumplings filled with a sweet mixture of khoya (reduced milk), coconut, nuts, and dried fruits, often flavoured with cardamom and saffron.

Thandai: A refreshing milk-based drink infused with almonds, pistachios, saffron, and spices like cardamom and fennel seeds, often spiked with bhang (cannabis paste) during Holi celebrations.

Puran Poli: A traditional sweet flatbread made with a filling of sweetened lentils, jaggery, and spices, rolled out into thin discs and cooked on a griddle, a specialty of Maharashtra and Gujarat.

Eid:

Eid al-Fitr and Eid al-Adha are important Islamic festivals celebrated by Muslims around the world. These festivals are marked by prayers, feasting, and the exchange of gifts. Traditional dishes are prepared to share with family and friends during Eid celebrations.

Biryani: Fragrant rice dish cooked with meat (such as chicken, mutton, or beef), aromatic spices, and herbs, a quintessential dish served during Eid festivities.

Sheer Khurma: A rich and creamy vermicelli pudding made with milk, dates, nuts, and saffron, flavoured with cardamom and rose water, a traditional dessert enjoyed on Eid al-Fitr.

Kebabs: Juicy and flavourful meat skewers made with minced meat (such as lamb or chicken) mixed with spices and grilled to perfection, often served as appetizers during Eid gatherings.

Christmas:

Christmas is celebrated by Christians across India with great enthusiasm and joy. Traditional Christmas dishes are prepared to mark the occasion, along with festive sweets and treats.

Plum Cake: A rich and moist fruitcake made with dried fruits, nuts, spices, and rum or brandy, a popular Christmas dessert in India.

Roast Turkey* A succulent whole turkey seasoned with herbs and spices, roasted until golden brown and served with gravy and cranberry sauce, a classic Christmas centerpiece.

Kulkuls: Deep-fried sweet dough curls made from a mixture of flour, sugar, and coconut milk, often flavoured with cardamom and rose water, a traditional Christmas treat in Goa and Kerala.

Street Food Favourites:

Explore the vibrant street food culture of India by featuring popular street food dishes from across the country. Include recipes for chaats, kebabs, dosas, vadas, and other street snacks.

Certainly! Street food in India is an integral part of the culinary landscape, offering a wide variety of flavourful and affordable dishes that are enjoyed by people of all ages. From savory snacks to sweet treats, street food reflects the diverse culinary traditions and cultural influences found across the country. Here's an elaborate list of famous street food favourites from different regions of India, that are loved by Foreign Nationals.

Pani Puri/Gol Gappe/Puchka (North India):

A popular street food snack consisting of hollow, crispy puris filled with spicy, tangy water (pani), boiled potatoes, chickpeas, and tamarind chutney.

Chole Bhature (North India):

A hearty and flavourful dish featuring spicy chickpea curry (chole) served with deep-fried, fluffy bread (bhature), often accompanied by pickles and onions.

Kathi Roll (North India):

A popular street food wrap originating from Kolkata, featuring skewered and grilled meat or paneer wrapped in a paratha or roti, along with onions, chutney, and spices.

Samosa (North India):

Triangular pastry filled with a spicy mixture of potatoes, peas, and spices, deep-fried until golden brown and crispy, often served with chutneys.

Vada Pav (West India, especially Mumbai):

A quintessential Mumbai Street food snack consisting of a spicy potato fritter (vada) sandwiched between pav (soft bread rolls), served with chutneys and fried green chilies.

Pav Bhaji (West India, especially Mumbai):

A flavourful and spicy vegetable mash (bhaji) made with mixed vegetables, tomatoes, onions, and spices, served with buttered pav (bread rolls) and garnished with onions, lemon, and cilantro.

Dabeli (West India, especially Gujarat):

A popular street food snack originating from Gujarat, featuring a spicy and tangy potato mixture stuffed inside a pav (soft bread roll), garnished with chutneys, sev, and pomegranate seeds.

Poha (West India):

A light and nutritious breakfast dish made from flattened rice (poha) sautéed with onions, mustard seeds, curry leaves, peanuts, and spices, often garnished with cilantro and lemon juice.

Dosa (South India):

A thin and crispy fermented crepe made from rice and lentil batter, served with various fillings such as potato masala, paneer, or cheese, accompanied by coconut chutney and sambar.

Idli (South India):

Soft and fluffy steamed rice cakes made from fermented rice and lentil batter, served with coconut chutney, sambar, and sometimes a spicy tomato chutney.

Bhelpuri (West India):

A tangy and crunchy snack made from puffed rice (murmura) mixed with chopped onions, tomatoes, boiled potatoes, peanuts, sev, and chutneys, served in a paper cone.

Chaat (Various regions):

A broad category of Savory snacks comprising a variety of dishes like Aloo Chaat (spicy potato snack), Papdi Chaat (crispy flour discs with toppings), and Sev Puri (crisp puris topped with chutneys, sev, and spices).

Kachori (Various regions):

Deep-fried, flaky pastry filled with a spicy mixture of lentils, peas, or potatoes, seasoned with spices like fennel, coriander, and ginger, often served with tamarind chutney.

Jalebi (Various regions):

Crispy and syrupy spiral-shaped sweets made from fermented batter deep-fried in circular shapes and soaked in sugar syrup, enjoyed as a popular dessert or snack.

Golgappa/Puchka/Pani Puri (Various regions):

Hollow, crispy puris filled with a spicy, tangy water (pani), boiled potatoes, chickpeas, and tamarind chutney, a beloved street food snack across India with regional variations in name and preparation.

Aloo Tikki Chaat (North India):

Spicy potato patties (aloo tikki) topped with tangy tamarind chutney, yogurt, and a sprinkle of chaat masala, garnished with chopped onions and cilantro.

Misal Pav (Maharashtra):

A spicy and tangy sprouted lentil curry (misal) served with pav (soft bread rolls), topped with farsan (crispy toppings), chopped onions, and lemon wedges.

Paddu/Paniyaram (South India):

Bite-sized Savory dumplings made from fermented rice and lentil batter, cooked in a special mold until crispy on the outside and soft on the inside, served with coconut chutney and sambar.

Chole Kulche (North India):

Spicy and tangy chickpea curry (chole) served with soft and fluffy kulcha (leavened bread), often accompanied by onions, green chilies, and pickle.

Mirchi Bajji (Andhra Pradesh):

Spicy green chilies dipped in a gram flour batter, deep-fried until crispy and golden brown, served hot with chutneys or a sprinkle of chaat masala.

Momo (North-East India/Tibetan):

Steamed or fried dumplings filled with a Savory mixture of vegetables, meat, or paneer, served with spicy dipping sauces like tomato chutney or momo sauce.

Jhal Muri (West Bengal):

A spicy and tangy snack made from puffed rice mixed with chopped onions, tomatoes, green chilies, coriander leaves, mustard oil, and a squeeze of lemon juice.

Churros (Goa/Spain):

Deep-fried dough pastry strips sprinkled with cinnamon sugar, served hot and crispy, often accompanied by chocolate sauce or dulce de leche for dipping.

Kothu Parotta (Tamil Nadu):

A popular street food dish made with shredded parotta (layered flatbread) stir-fried with vegetables, eggs, and spices, often served with a side of raita or curry.

Dabeli (Gujarat):

A spicy and tangy potato filling sandwiched between buttered pav (soft bread rolls), garnished with peanuts, pomegranate seeds, sev, and chutneys like tamarind and garlic.

These street foods offer a wide range of Flavors, textures, and regional influences, adding to the vibrant tapestry of Indian street food culture.

Family Favourites:

Recipes that have been cherished by Indian families for generations are the family favourites. These can be comfort foods, childhood favourites, or dishes with sentimental value.

Family favourites are dishes that hold a special place in the hearts of families across India and the ingredients are mostly prepared at home. These are often recipes that have been passed down through generations, cherished for their comforting Flavors and memories associated with shared meals. Foreign Nationals choosing to opt for Home Stays across India can have a tase of these foods wherever they stay.

Rajma Chawal (North India):

A beloved Punjabi dish featuring red kidney beans cooked in a thick tomato-based gravy, served with steamed rice (chawal), often accompanied by sliced onions and a dollop of yogurt.

Dal Tadka (North India):

A comforting and nutritious dish made with yellow lentils (dal), tempered with ghee, cumin seeds, garlic, and spices like turmeric and red chili powder, served with rice or roti.

Paneer Butter Masala (North India):

Soft paneer (Indian cottage cheese) cubes simmered in a creamy and rich tomato-based gravy, flavoured with butter, cream, and a blend of aromatic spices, served with naan or rice.

Aloo Gobi (North India):

A classic vegetarian dish made with potatoes (aloo) and cauliflower (gobi) cooked with onions, tomatoes, ginger, garlic, and spices like turmeric, cumin, and coriander, served with roti or paratha.

Khichdi (All over India):

A wholesome one-pot meal made with rice and lentils, cooked together with vegetables and spices, often served with a dollop of ghee, yogurt, or pickle on the side, enjoyed by families across India.

Sambhar (South India):

A flavourful and tangy lentil-based stew made with vegetables like drumsticks, pumpkin, and eggplant, seasoned with a special blend of spices and tamarind, served with rice or idli.

Rasam (South India):

A comforting and aromatic soup (used as an appetizer) made with tamarind juice, tomatoes, garlic, cumin, black pepper, and other spices, often served as a palate cleanser or with rice and papad.

Puliyogare (South India):

A tangy and spicy rice dish made with tamarind paste, spices, and peanuts, mixed with cooked rice, often served as prasadam (offering) in temples and enjoyed during festivals.

Bhindi Masala (North India):

Okra (bhindi) cooked with onions, tomatoes, ginger, garlic, and spices like turmeric, coriander, and garam masala, creating a flavourful and aromatic dish served with roti or rice.

Bisi Bele Bath (Karnataka):

A hearty and flavourful rice dish made with rice, lentils, mixed vegetables, tamarind, and a special spice blend, cooked together to create a delicious one-pot meal.

Butter Chicken (North India):

Tender pieces of chicken cooked in a creamy and flavourful tomato-based gravy, enriched with butter, cream, and aromatic spices, often served with naan or rice.

Hyderabadi Biryani (South India):

Fragrant basmati rice cooked with marinated meat (usually chicken or mutton), caramelized onions, yogurt, and a blend of spices, layered together and cooked to perfection, served with raita.

Dhokla (Gujarat):

Steamed Savory cakes made from fermented batter of rice and chickpea flour, flavoured with green chilies, ginger, and tempered with mustard seeds and curry leaves, served with green chutney.

Pav Bhaji (West India, especially Mumbai):

A spicy and flavourful vegetable mash (bhaji) made with mixed vegetables, tomatoes, onions, and spices, served with buttered pav (bread rolls) and garnished with onions, lemon, and cilantro.

Malai Kofta (North India):

Soft and creamy paneer (Indian cottage cheese) and potato dumplings (koftas) cooked in a rich and creamy tomato-based gravy, flavoured with nuts, cream, and aromatic spices, served with naan or rice.

Matar Paneer (North India):

Paneer (Indian cottage cheese) and green peas (matar) cooked in a flavourful tomato-based gravy, seasoned with spices like garam masala, cumin, and coriander, served with roti or rice.

Chole Bhature (North India):

Spicy and tangy chickpea curry (chole) served with deep-fried, fluffy bread (bhature), often accompanied by pickles and onions, a popular street food and family favourite.

Rava Upma (South India):

A quick and nutritious breakfast dish made with roasted semolina (rava) cooked with onions, mustard seeds, curry leaves, and spices, often served with coconut chutney or sugar.

Kadhi Pakora (North India):

A tangy and creamy yogurt-based curry (kadhi) with crispy gram flour (besan) dumplings (pakoras), flavoured with fenugreek seeds, cumin, and turmeric, served with steamed rice.

Mughlai Paratha (North India):

Flaky and stuffed paratha filled with a rich and flavourful mixture of minced meat, onions, spices, and herbs, pan-fried until golden brown and crispy, served with yogurt or chutney.

These family favourite dishes continue to bring joy and satisfaction to dining tables across India, with their comforting Flavors and timeless appeal, as they reflect the diverse culinary traditions across the country.

Vegetarian Delights

India is known for its rich vegetarian culinary traditions. Vegetarian delights are dishes that cater to the preferences of vegetarians, highlighting the rich and diverse culinary traditions of vegetarian cuisine in India. Here's an elaboration along with some names of vegetarian dishes:

Palak Paneer:

A classic North Indian dish made with spinach (palak) puree cooked with paneer (Indian cottage cheese) cubes, onions, tomatoes, and spices, enriched with cream and butter.

Aloo Gobi:

A popular North Indian dish featuring potatoes (aloo) and cauliflower (gobi) cooked with onions, tomatoes, ginger, garlic, and spices, creating a flavourful and comforting dish.

Baingan Bharta:

Roasted and mashed eggplant (baingan) cooked with onions, tomatoes, green chilies, and spices, garnished with cilantro, creating a smoky and flavourful vegetarian delight.

Dal Makhani:

A creamy and indulgent lentil dish made with black lentils (urad dal) and kidney beans (rajma), cooked with tomatoes, ginger, garlic, and aromatic spices, finished with cream and butter.

Chana Masala:

A spicy and tangy chickpea (chana) curry cooked with onions, tomatoes, ginger, garlic, and a blend of aromatic spices, garnished with cilantro, perfect for pairing with rice or roti.

Paneer Tikka Masala:

Marinated paneer (Indian cottage cheese) cubes grilled to perfection and cooked in a creamy and flavourful tomato-based gravy, seasoned with spices and finished with cream and butter.

Matar Paneer:

Paneer (Indian cottage cheese) and green peas (matar) cooked in a rich and flavourful tomato-based gravy, seasoned with spices like garam masala, cumin, and coriander, a North Indian favourite.

Vegetable Biryani:

Fragrant basmati rice cooked with an assortment of mixed vegetables, spices, and herbs, layered together and cooked until fragrant and flavourful, perfect for special occasions and gatherings.

Mixed Vegetable Curry:

A medley of mixed vegetables like carrots, peas, potatoes, cauliflower, and beans cooked in a spiced tomato-based gravy, creating a hearty and satisfying vegetarian dish.

Masoor Dal:

Red lentils (masoor dal) cooked with onions, tomatoes, garlic, and spices, tempered with ghee, cumin seeds, and dried red chilies, creating a comforting and nutritious dal dish.

These vegetarian delights showcase the versatility and flavour profile of vegetarian cuisine in India, offering a wide range of options for those who prefer meat-free meals. From creamy curries to hearty rice dishes, these dishes are sure to delight vegetarians and non-vegetarians alike.

Accompaniments and Condiments:

"Accompaniments and Condiments" refer to additional items (toppings) that are served alongside main dishes to complement and enhance their Flavors. These can range from simple sauces and dips to more complex side dishes. Here's an elaboration on some common accompaniments and condiments in Indian cuisine:

Chutneys:

Chutneys are flavourful sauces made from fruits, vegetables, herbs, and spices. They can be sweet, Savory, or spicy and are often served as accompaniments to snacks, appetizers, and main dishes. Common varieties include mint chutney, tamarind chutney, and coconut chutney.

Raita:

Raita is a yogurt-based condiment that is commonly served alongside spicy Indian dishes to balance their Flavors and cool the palate. It is made by mixing yogurt with chopped vegetables (such as cucumber, tomato, or onion), herbs (such as cilantro or mint), and spices.

Pickle (Achaar):

Pickles, or achaar, are preserved fruits or vegetables that are marinated in oil, vinegar, or brine with spices and seasonings. They add a tangy and spicy flavour to meals and are often served as condiments or side dishes.

Papadum/Papad:

Papadum, also known as papad, is a thin and crispy Indian cracker made from lentil, chickpea, or rice flour. It is often served as an appetizer or accompaniment to meals, either plain or roasted, and can be accompanied by chutneys or pickles.

Naan/Roti:

Naan and roti are traditional Indian bread made from wheat flour and cooked in a tandoor (clay oven) or on a griddle. They are often served alongside curries, dals, and other main dishes to soak up the flavourful sauces.

Dosa/Idli

Dosa and idli are South Indian fermented rice and lentil-based dishes, typically served with coconut chutney, sambar (spicy lentil soup), and various accompaniments like potato masala or tomato chutney.

Salads:

Salads made from fresh vegetables, fruits, and herbs are commonly served as accompaniments to Indian meals. They provide a refreshing contrast to spicy and rich dishes and can be dressed with lemon juice, chaat masala, or yogurt-based dressings.

Ghee:

Ghee, or clarified butter, is often used as a condiment or flavouring agent in Indian cuisine. It adds richness and depth of flavour to dishes and is drizzled over rice, lentils, and vegetables.

Lime or Lemon Wedges:

Lime or lemon wedges are commonly served as a garnish or accompaniment to Indian dishes. They provide a burst of citrusy freshness and can be squeezed over curries, biryanis, and grilled meats.

Fresh Herbs:

Fresh herbs like cilantro (coriander), mint, and curry leaves are used to garnish and flavour Indian dishes. They add brightness and aroma to meals and can be sprinkled over curries, rice dishes, and salads.

These accompaniments and condiments play a crucial role in Indian cuisine, adding layers of flavour, texture, and freshness to meals and enhancing the overall dining experience.

Menu Planning:

Menu planning is a crucial aspect of culinary preparation, whether it's for everyday meals at home, special occasions, or professional cooking in restaurants and catering services. It involves thoughtful consideration of various factors to create a well-balanced and satisfying dining experience. Here's a detailed explanation and elaboration on menu planning:

1. **Identifying the Purpose**: The first step in menu planning is to identify the purpose of the meal. Are you planning for:

A casual family dinner Formal dinner party Themed event

Understanding the purpose will help determine the tone, style, and complexity of the menu.

2. **Understanding Dietary Preferences and Restrictions**: It's essential to consider the dietary preferences, restrictions, and allergies of the guests or diners. This includes vegetarian, vegan, gluten-free, and dairy-free options to accommodate everyone's needs.

3. **Balancing Flavors and Textures**: A well-planned menu should offer a balance of Flavors, textures, and colours to create a harmonious dining experience. Consider incorporating a variety of tastes, such as sweet, sour, salty, bitter, and umami, as well as different textures like crunchy, creamy, and chewy.

4. **Seasonal and Local Ingredients:** Utilizing seasonal and locally sourced ingredients not only ensures freshness and quality but also supports local farmers and reduces the carbon footprint of the meal. Incorporating seasonal produce and ingredients adds variety and vibrancy to the menu.

5. **Considering the Flow of the Meal**: Plan the menu to flow seamlessly from appetizers to mains to desserts, with each course complementing the next. Gradually build Flavors and intensity throughout the meal, starting with lighter dishes and progressing to richer and more complex Flavors.

6. **Offering Variety:** A well-rounded menu should offer a variety of dishes to cater to different tastes and preferences. Include options for appetizers, soups, salads, mains, sides, and desserts, as well as vegetarian and non-vegetarian options, to ensure there's something for everyone.

7. **Creating Visual Appeal:** Presentation is key to a memorable dining experience. Consider the visual presentation of each dish, including plating techniques, garnishes, and serving vessels, to enhance the aesthetic appeal of the meal.

8. **Striking a Balance Between Familiarity and Innovation**: While it's essential to offer familiar dishes that are comforting and crowd-pleasing, don't be afraid to introduce innovative and creative elements to surprise and delight diners. Balance traditional recipes with modern twists and innovative flavour combinations.

9. **Practical Considerations**: Consider practical aspects such as cooking equipment, available kitchen space, and timing constraints when planning the menu. Choose dishes that can be prepared in advance, scaled up or down as needed, and executed efficiently to ensure a smooth dining experience.

10. **Seeking Feedback and Iteration:** Finally, seek feedback from guests or diners after the meal to evaluate what worked well and what could be improved. Use this feedback to iterate and refine future menus, continually striving to create memorable dining experiences.

Overall, effective menu planning requires careful consideration of various factors, including dietary preferences, seasonal ingredients, flavor balance, presentation, and practical considerations. By following these guidelines and principles, you can create well-balanced and satisfying menus that cater to the tastes and preferences of your audience, whether at home or in a professional setting.

Culinary Stories and Anecdotes:

Once upon a time, in the bustling streets of Chennai, a young man named **Prabhakar (Author)** embarked on a culinary journey that would forever change his life. Born and raised in the heart of South India, Prabhakar's palate was accustomed to the bold Flavors and aromatic spices of his homeland. However, it wasn't until he ventured to the vibrant dynamic city of New Delhi for work where his culinary adventure truly began!!!

Fresh out of college at the **age of 22**, Prabhakar found himself navigating the fast-paced life of a bachelor in the bustling capital city New Delhi. With little knowledge of cooking and a penchant for street food, he relied heavily on the tantalizing aromas and Flavors wafting from roadside stalls to satisfy his hunger.

But as the years passed, Prabhakar's reliance on street food took its toll on his health. A lack of vegetables in his diet left him susceptible to frequent bouts of illness, prompting him to rethink his approach to food. At the **age of 24**, fuelled by a desire for better health and a newfound curiosity, Prabhakar took his first tentative steps into the world of cooking.

Armed with determination and a willingness to learn, Prabhakar embarked on a culinary journey that would transform him from a novice cook into a skilled chef. With each dish he mastered, from fragrant biryanis to hearty curries, Prabhakar's confidence in the kitchen grew.

At the **age of 29**, Prabhakar's life took another turn as he tied the knot and embarked on a new chapter with his wife. Together, they explored the vast and diverse world of Indian cuisine, experimenting with recipes from North to South and everything in between.

But it wasn't just the Flavors of India that captivated Prabhakar – it was the joy of sharing his culinary creations with others. Whether cooking for family, friends, or guests, Prabhakar found immense satisfaction in seeing others enjoy his food.

Amidst his culinary adventures, Prabhakar developed a deep affection for certain iconic dishes that held a special place in his heart. From the indulgent delights of Choley Bhaturey and the smoky allure of Paneer Tikka to the crispy perfection of Onion Kachori and the irresistible charm of Ram Laddu, each bite carried memories of cherished moments and Flavors that resonated with his soul.

He found solace in the simplicity of Makki ka Roti paired with a dollop of creamy butter, while the pillowy softness of Butter Naan never failed to comfort him. And on lazy evenings, there was nothing quite like the crunchy goodness of Pesarattu and the crispy goodness of Onion Pakoras to satisfy his cravings. These dishes weren't just meals; they were gateways to nostalgia, joy, and the timeless pleasures of good food shared with loved ones. His signature dish is Veg. Biryani.

Fuelled by a passion for cooking and a thirst for adventure, Prabhakar's culinary journey didn't end in the kitchen. As an avid traveller, he sought out new and exciting Flavors in every corner of the country, expanding his culinary repertoire with each new discovery.

Today, **Prabhakar** is more than just a home chef – he's a culinary maestro, known for his exquisite dishes and unwavering commitment to quality. And though his standards may be high, his love for cooking and sharing food with others remains undiminished. This is the story of Prabhakar – a journey of passion, perseverance, and the transformative power of food.

Okay, that's my story and its time now to get into Recipes as I am feeling hungry and would invite you to my Kitchen, come lets enjoy the flavourful dishes!!!!

Welcome to the heart of our culinary journey !!!!! the recipes section!

Get ready to embark on a flavourful adventure that will tantalize your taste buds and transport you to the vibrant streets of India. Each recipe is a celebration of tradition, innovation, and the rich tapestry of Indian Flavors.

From aromatic curries to mouthwatering street food delights, our collection offers something for every palate and occasion. Whether you're a seasoned chef or a novice in the kitchen, these recipes are crafted to inspire and delight, guiding you through the intricate steps with ease and excitement.

So, grab your apron, sharpen your knives, and let's dive into the magical world of Indian cuisine together. Get ready to unleash your inner chef and create unforgettable culinary masterpieces that will dazzle and delight your family and friends. Let the cooking adventures begin!

Menu Card

Breakfast Dishes

1. Masala Dosa
2. Parota Kurma
3. Aloo Parota
4. Poha
5. Medu Vada
6. Choley Bhature

Lunch Dishes

1. Butter Chicken
2. Briyani
3. Paneer Tikka Masala
4. Rogan Josh (Mutton Curry)
5. Palak Paneer
6. Bisi Bele Bath
7. Tandoori Chicken
8. Dal Makhni
9. Kadi Pakora

Dinner Dishes

1. Veg Fried Rice
2. Dum Aloo
3. Suji (Rava) Upma
4. Fish Curry with Rice
5. Dal Fry

Recipes of Famous Indian Breakfast Dishes

Masala Dosa

SERVINGS: 4   **PREPPING TIME: 15 MIN**   **COOKING TIME: 30 MIN**

Ingredients

- Dosa batter: Approx 4 cups
- Potatoes: 4 medium-sized
  Onions: 2 large onions, finely chopped.
- Green chilies: 2-3 green chilies, finely chopped
- Mustard seeds: 1 teaspoon
- Curry leaves: 8-10 leaves
- Turmeric powder: 1/2 teaspoon
- Salt: As per taste
- Oil: For cooking dosas and sautéing the filling, approximately 4-5 tablespoons

For Coconut CHutney

- Grated Coconut: ½ cup
- Fresh coriander leaves: 1/2 cup
- Green chilies: 2 (adjust according to spice preference)
- Garlic cloves: 2-3 (optional)
- Ginger: 1 small piece
- Salt: As per taste
- Water: 2-3 tablespoons (adjust for desired consistency)

Directions

- Prepare a filling by boiling and mashing potatoes.

- In a pan, heat oil, and add mustard seeds, curry leaves, chopped onions, and green chilies. Add turmeric powder and salt, then mix in mashed potatoes.

- Spread dosa batter thinly on a hot griddle or a non-stick tawa.
- Sprinkle oil, and spread the potato filling over one-half of the dosa.
- Fold the dosa over the filling and cook until crisp.

- Serve hot with coconut chutney and sambar.

- Rinse the coriander leaves under running water to remove any dirt.
- In a blender or food processor, combine the coriander leaves, coconut, green chilies, ginger, and salt.
- Blend the ingredients until you get a smooth paste. If the mixture is too thick, add water gradually to achieve the desired consistency.
- Taste the chutney and adjust the seasoning according to your preference. You can add more salt, lemon juice, or green chilies for extra spice.
- Serve the chutney as a condiment along with Dosa or other snacks like samosas, pakoras, dosas, or sandwiches.

Parota Kurma

SERVINGS: 2　　　**PREPPING TIME: 15 MIN**　　　**COOKING TIME: 30 MIN**

Ingredients

For Parota

- 2 cups all-purpose flour (maida)
- 1 tablespoon ghee (clarified butter)
- Water
- Salt
-

For Kurma

- Mixed vegetables (carrots, peas, potatoes, beans)
- Onion
- Tomato
- Ginger-garlic paste
- Coconut milk
- Kurma masala powder
- Oil
- Salt
- Coriander leaves for garnish

Directions

- In a mixing bowl, add the all-purpose flour, ghee, and a pinch of salt. Mix well.
- Gradually add water and knead the dough until it is soft and smooth.
- Divide the dough into equal-sized balls and let them rest for about 15-20 minutes.
- Take one dough ball and roll it out into a thin disc.
- Brush the disc with ghee and sprinkle some flour over it.
- Fold the disc into pleats, similar to folding a paper fan.
- Coil the pleated dough into a spiral shape and tuck the end underneath.
- Flatten the coiled dough slightly and roll it out into a thin parota.
- Heat a griddle or tawa over medium heat and cook the parota on both sides until golden brown spots appear.
- Remove from the griddle and serve hot with kurma

- Heat oil in a pan and sauté onions until golden brown.
- Add ginger-garlic paste and sauté until the raw smell disappears.
- Add chopped tomatoes and cook until they turn mushy.
- Add mixed vegetables and cook until they are partially cooked.
- Add kurma masala powder and salt to taste. Mix well.
- Pour in coconut milk and simmer until the vegetables are cooked through.
- Garnish with chopped coriander leaves.
- Serve hot with Malabar Parota.

Aloo Parota

SERVINGS: 4   **PREPPING TIME: 15 MIN**   **COOKING TIME: 30 MIN**

Ingredients

- Whole wheat flour 4 cups
- Potatoes - 6 Nos.
- Green chilies
- Cumin seeds
- Coriander leaves
- Garam masala
- Salt
- Ghee or Oil
- Butter

Directions

- Prepare a soft dough using whole wheat flour, water, and salt.
- For the filling, boil, peel, and mash potatoes. Mix with chopped green chilies, cumin seeds, coriander leaves, garam masala, and salt.
- Roll out small portions of dough, place a portion of filling in the center, seal, and roll into a paratha.
- Cook the paratha on a hot griddle with ghee or oil until golden brown on both sides.
- Serve hot with yogurt or pickle.

Aloo Parota is taken along with Curd, Pickle and Butter for added taste.
It gives a Crispy, flaky exterior with a spicy and flavorful potato filling.

Variants: Gobi Paratha, Paneer Paratha, Methi Paratha, Palak Paratha, Mooli Paratha, Pyaaz Paratha, Mix Veg. Paratha, Chana Dal Paratha, and Cheese Paratha.

Poha

SERVINGS: 4 **PREPPING TIME: 5 MIN** **COOKING TIME: 15 MIN**

Ingredients

- Flattened rice (poha)
- Potatoes
- Peanuts
- Onions
- Green chilies
- Mustard seeds
- Curry leaves
- Turmeric powder
- Lemon juice
- Coriander leaves
- Salt
- Oil

Directions

- Rinse poha under running water and drain well.
- Heat oil in a pan, add mustard seeds, peanuts, chopped onions, green chilies, and curry leaves.
- Add diced potatoes, turmeric powder, and salt. Cook until potatoes are tender.
- Mix in drained poha and cook until heated through.
- Finish with a squeeze of lemon juice and chopped coriander leaves.
- Serve hot garnished with more coriander leaves.

Taste : Light and fluffy poha with a tangy and spicy flavour profile.

For variance you can boil our favorite vegetables and add to poha.

This is the easiest Breakfast that can be made in 15 Minutes yet healthy.

Medu Vada

SERVINGS: 4   **PREPPING TIME: 15 MIN**   **COOKING TIME: 15 MIN**

Ingredients

- Urad dal 3 cups
- Green chilies
- Ginger
- Curry leaves
- Pepper
- Cumin seeds
- Salt
- Oil for frying

Directions

- Soak urad dal for at least 8 hours, then grind to a smooth batter with green chilies, ginger, curry leaves, pepper, and cumin seeds.
- Add salt and mix well. The batter should be thick and fluffy.
- Heat oil in a deep frying pan. Wet your hands, take a portion of the batter, shape it into a donut, and carefully slide it into the hot oil.
- Fry until golden brown and crispy. Remove and drain excess oil on paper towels.
- Serve hot with coconut chutney and sambar.

Taste : Crispy.

For added taste, you can add nicely chopped onion and chili in the batter before frying.
Other Variants : Masala Vada, Gobi Vada, Pepper Vada, Palak Vada, Thayir Vada, Rava Vada.

Choley Bhature

<u>SERVINGS: 4</u>   PREPPING TIME: 30 MIN   COOKING TIME: 60 MIN

Ingredients

- Chickpeas: 1.5 cups, soaked overnight and boiled
- Onions: 2 medium, finely chopped
- Tomatoes: 2 finely chopped
- Ginger-garlic paste: 1 tbs.
- Green chilies: 2, slit
- Cumin seeds: 1 teaspoon
- Coriander powder: 2 teaspoons
- Cumin powder: 1 teaspoon
- Red chili powder: 1 teaspoon
- Turmeric powder: 1/2 teaspoon
- Garam masala: 1 teaspoon
- Amchur (dry mango powder): 1 teaspoon
- Salt: to taste
- Oil: 2 tablespoons
- Water: as needed
- Coriander leaves: for garnish

Tip-1 : I add tea decoction while boiling chickpeas to give it a restaurant color.

Tip-2 : You can add rice to choley and have it as a lunch.

Directions

- Heat oil in a pan. Add cumin seeds and let them splutter.
- Add onions and sauté until golden brown. Add ginger-garlic paste and green chilies, sauté for a minute.
- Add chopped tomatoes and cook until they soften.
- Add all the spice powders (coriander, cumin, red chili, turmeric, garam masala, and amchur) and salt. Cook until oil separates from the masala.
- Add boiled chickpeas and enough water to get the desired consistency. Simmer for 15-20 minutes.
- Garnish with chopped coriander leaves.

<u>For Bhature ingredients and preparation is as below :</u>

- All-purpose flour (Maida): 2 cups, Yogurt: 1/4 cup, Baking powder: 1/2 teaspoon, Baking soda: 1/4 teaspoon, Sugar: 1 teaspoon, Salt: 1/2 teaspoon, Oil: 2 tablespoons + for deep frying
- Water: as needed to knead the dough.

<u>Preparation</u>

- In a large bowl, mix flour, baking powder, baking soda, sugar, and salt.
- Add yogurt and 2 tablespoons of oil. Mix well.
- Gradually add water and knead into a soft dough. Cover and let it rest for at least 2 hours.
- Divide the dough into small balls. Roll each ball into a thin oval shape.
- Heat oil in a deep frying pan. Deep fry each bhatura until puffed up and golden brown on both sides. Drain on paper towels

Top Indian Lunch Dishes:

Butter Chicken

SERVINGS: 4   **PREPPING TIME: 30 MIN**   **COOKING TIME: 60 MIN**

Ingredients

- Chicken 2 Nos. full
- Butter
- Onion
- Tomato
- Cream
- Yogurt
- Ginger-garlic paste
- Garam masala
- Chili powder- Kasuri methi (dried fenugreek leaves)
- Salt
- Oil

Directions

- Marinate chicken pieces in yogurt, ginger-garlic paste, and spices and keep it for 30 minutes.
- Grill or roast until cooked.
- Prepare a sauce by sautéing onions, tomatoes, and spices until soft. Blend into a smooth paste.
- Heat butter in a pan, add the paste, cream, and kasuri methi. Simmer until the sauce thickens.
- Add grilled chicken pieces to the sauce and simmer until well coated.
- Serve hot with rice Butter Roti or naan.

Taste: Creamy and rich sauce with tender chicken pieces, mildly spiced with a hint of sweetness

Tips: It is the gravy mixture of onion and tomato along with masala that makes the tasty

Briyani

SERVINGS: 4   **PREPPING TIME: 45 MIN**   **COOKING TIME: 60 MIN**

Ingredients

- Basmati rice 4 Cups
- Chicken, mutton, or vegetables
- Yogurt
- Onion
- Tomato
- Ginger-garlic paste
- Biryani masala
- Saffron
- Mint leaves
- Coriander leaves
- Ghee
- Salt

Directions

- Cut the desired vegetables needed and half Boil them and stain.
- (or) Marinate meat in yogurt, and spices, and add ginger-garlic paste. Cook until partially done.
- Parboil rice with whole spices and salt. Drain.
- Take a cooker and add Ghee, cashew, and bay leaves, and chopped ginger, garlic, and green chili.
- Add Briyani Masala Curd and tomato paste to form a thick gravy.
- Start layering by pouring cooked vegetables or cooked meat in the first layer and on the second layer, pour half-boiled basmati rice, spread fried onions, mint leaves, and saffron-infused milk. Repeat this as several layers until stock lasts.
- Finally, seal and cook on low heat until the rice is fluffy and aromatic.
- Serve hot with raita or salan.

Tips : Add Kevda or Rose Water while boiling the rice to have a fantastic aroma.

This is my signature dish and i make it with full love and dedication !!!

Paneer Tikka Masala

<u>SERVINGS: 4</u>   PREPPING TIME: 45 MIN   COOKING TIME: 30 MIN

Ingredients

- Paneer (Indian cottage cheese) 500 Gms
- Bell peppers
- Onion - 6
- Tomato - 6
- Cream
- Yogurt
- Ginger-garlic paste
- Garam masala
- Chili powder
- Kasuri methi
- Salt
- Oil

Directions

- Marinate paneer and vegetables in yogurt, allspices, and ginger-garlic paste. Grill or roast until golden brown.
- Prepare a sauce by sautéing onions, tomatoes, and spices until soft. Blend into a smooth paste.
- Heat oil in a pan, add the paste, cream, and kasuri methi. Simmer until the sauce thickens.
- Add grilled paneer and vegetables to the sauce and simmer until well coated.
- Serve hot with naan or rice.

Taste: Creamy and flavorful sauce with grilled paneer and vegetables, mildly spicy with a hint of tanginess.

Tips : Grilled Paneer (Cottage cheese) also can be had separately as evening snack.

Rogan Josh (Mutton Curry)

SERVINGS: 4   **PREPPING TIME: 45 MIN**   **COOKING TIME: 30 MIN**

Ingredients

- Mutton - 2 Kgs
- Onion -6
- Tomato-6
- Yogurt
- Ginger-garlic paste
- Garam masala
- Chili powder
- Saffron
- Cream
- Kasuri methi
- Oil
- Salt
-

Directions

- Marinate mutton in yogurt, spices, and ginger-garlic paste. Cook until tender.
- Prepare a sauce by sautéing onions, tomatoes, and spices until soft. Blend into a smooth paste.
- Heat oil in a pan, add the paste, cream, and kasuri methi. Simmer until the sauce thickens.
- Add cooked mutton to the sauce and simmer until well coated.
- Serve hot with rice or naan.

Taste: Rich and aromatic sauce with tender mutton pieces, spicy and flavorful with a hint of saffron.

Palak Paneer

SERVINGS: 4   **PREPPING TIME: 45 MIN**   **COOKING TIME: 30 MIN**

Ingredients

- Paneer
- Spinach
- Onion
- Tomato
- Ginger-garlic paste
- Garam masala
- Chili powder
- Cream
- Kasuri methi
- Oil
- Salt

Directions

- Blanch spinach leaves, then blend into a smooth puree.
- Sauté onions, tomatoes, and spices until soft. Add spinach puree and cook until flavors meld.
- Fry Paneer cut into cubes in oil
- Add cubed paneer and simmer until well combined.
- Finish with cream and kasuri methi.
- Serve hot with rice or naan.

Taste: Creamy spinach sauce with soft paneer cubes, mildly spiced and earthy in flavor.

Bisi Bele Bath

SERVINGS: 4　　　　**PREPPING TIME: 45 MIN**　　　　**COOKING TIME: 30 MIN**

Ingredients

For Masala

- Coriander seeds: 2 tablespoons
- Chana dal 1 tbs
- Urad dal (split black gm): 1 tbs
- Cumin seeds: 1 teaspoon
- Fenugreek seeds: 1/2 tbs
- Dry red chilies: 4-5
- Cinnamon stick: 1-inch piece
- Cloves: 3-4, Cardamom pods:
- Grated coconut: 2 tbs

For Bisi Bele Bath

- Rice: 1 cup
- Toor dal 1/2 cup
- Mixed veg. (carrots, beans, peas, potatoes): 1 cup, chopped
- Tamarind paste: 1 tablespoon
- Turmeric powder: 1/2 tbs
- Salt: to taste, Water: 4-5 cups
- Ghee (clarified butter): 2 tbs
- Mustard seeds: 1 teaspoon, Curry leaves: a few
- Cashew nuts: 2 tablespoons
- Fresh coriander leaves:

Directions

For Masala

- Dry roast all the ingredients for the bisi bele bath powder (except coconut) in a pan until fragrant and lightly browned.
- Let the roasted spices cool down completely.
- Grind the roasted spices along with grated coconut (if using) into a fine powder. Set aside.

For Bisi Bele Bath

- Wash rice and toor dal together. Soak them in water for 30 minutes.
- In a pressure cooker, add the soaked rice and dal along with chopped vegetables, tamarind paste, jaggery or sugar, turmeric powder, salt, and water.
- Pressure cook for 3-4 whistles or until rice and dal are cooked and vegetables are tender.
- Once the pressure releases, open the cooker and add the prepared bisi bele bath powder. Mix well.
- Heat ghee in a small pan. Add mustard seeds and let them splutter. Add cashew nuts (if using) and curry leaves. Fry until cashews turn golden brown.
- Pour the tempered ghee mixture over the bisi bele bath. Mix well.
- Garnish with freshly chopped coriander leaves

Tandoori Chicken

SERVINGS: 4　　　　**PREPPING TIME: 45 MIN**　　　　**COOKING TIME: 30 MIN**

Ingredients

- Chicken
- Yogurt
- Ginger-garlic paste
- Tandoori masala
- Chili powder
- Lemon juice
- Kasuri methi
- Oil
- Salt

Directions

- Marinate chicken pieces in yogurt, spices, and ginger-garlic paste.
- Refrigerate for a few hours.
- Grill or roast marinated chicken until cooked and charred.
- Sprinkle with lemon juice and kasuri methi.
- Serve hot with naan or mint chutney.

Taste: Smoky and flavorful grilled chicken, spicy and tangy with a hint of charred aroma.

Dal Makhni

SERVINGS: 4   **PREPPING TIME: 45 MIN**   **COOKING TIME: 30 MIN**

Ingredients

- Black lentils (urad dal)
- Kidney beans (rajma)
- Onion
- Tomato
- Ginger-garlic paste
- Garam masala
- Cream
- Butter
- Kasuri methi
- Oil
- Salt
-

Directions

- Soak Lentils and kidney beans at least for 8 hours.
- Fry Onion, tomato, spices, and ginger garlic paste and grind it into a paste.
- Cook-soaked lentils and kidney beans with the paste
- Finish with cream, butter, and kasuri methi.
- Serve hot with steamed rice or naan.

Kadi Pakora

SERVINGS: 4   **PREPPING TIME: 15 MIN**   **COOKING TIME: 30 MIN**

Ingredients

For Pakora

- Besan (gram flour): 1 cup
- Onions: 1, finely chopped
- Green chilies: 2, finely chopped
- coriander leaves: 2 tbs chopped
- Ajwain (carom seeds): 1/2 tbs
- Baking soda: 1/4 teaspoon
- Salt: to taste
- Water: as needed for batter
- Oil: for deep frying

For Kadi

- Sour yogurt: 1 cup
- Besan (gram flour): 2 tbs
- Water: 3 cups
- Turmeric powder: 1/2 teaspoon
- Red chili powder: 1/2 teaspoon
- Salt: to taste
- Mustard seeds: 1 teaspoon
- Fenugreek seeds: 1/2 teaspoon
- Curry leaves: a few
- Asafoetida (hing): 1/4 teaspoon
- Oil: 2 tablespoons
- Fresh coriander leaves:

Directions

- In a mixing bowl, add besan, salt to taste, turmeric, and red chili powder. Now beat the mixture for 5 minutes.
- Add chopped onions, green chilies, coriander leaves, ajwain, and baking soda.
- Heat oil in a deep frying pan. Drop small portions of the batter into the hot oil and fry until golden brown and crispy.
- Remove the pakoras from the oil and drain them on paper towels to remove excell oil and set aside.

- In a bowl, whisk together sour yogurt, besan, water, turmeric powder, red chili powder, and salt until smooth.
- Heat oil in a deep pan. Add mustard seeds and let them splutter. Add fenugreek seeds, curry leaves, and asafoetida. Saute for a few seconds.
- Pour the yogurt mixture into the pan and mix well.
- Cook the kadhi on medium heat, stirring continuously, until it comes to a boil.
- Reduce the heat and simmer the kadhi for 15-20 minutes, stirring occasionally, until it thickens slightly.
- Add the prepared pakoras to the kadhi and simmer for another 5 minutes to allow the flavors to meld together.
- Garnish with freshly chopped coriander leaves.

Veg. Fried Rice

SERVINGS: 4   **PREPPING TIME: 15 MIN**   **COOKING TIME: 30 MIN**

Ingredients

- Cooked rice: 2 cups (preferably leftover rice, cooled)
- Mixed vegetables (carrots, bell peppers, peas, corn): 1 cup, finely chopped
- Onion: 1 medium, finely chopped
- Garlic: 2 cloves, minced
- Ginger: 1 teaspoon, minced
- Green onions (spring onions): 2 stalks, chopped
- Soy sauce: 2 tablespoons
- Sesame oil: 1 tablespoon
- Vegetable oil: 2 tablespoons
- Salt: to taste
- Black pepper powder: 1/2 teaspoon
- White vinegar: 1 teaspoon (optional)
- Red chili sauce or Sriracha: 1 teaspoon (optional)
- Eggs: 2, beaten (optional)
- Fresh coriander leaves: for garnish (optional)

Directions

- If using leftover rice, ensure it is cooled completely. If cooking fresh rice, cook it according to package instructions and allow it to cool down before using.
- Fluff the cooked rice with a fork to break up any clumps. Set aside.

For Fred Rice

- Heat vegetable oil in a large pan or wok over medium-high heat.
- Add minced garlic and ginger to the hot oil and sauté for a minute until fragrant.
- Add chopped onions and cook until they turn translucent.
- Add mixed vegetables to the pan and stir-fry for 3-4 minutes until they are tender-crisp.
- Push the vegetables to one side of the pan and pour the beaten eggs into the other side. Scramble the eggs until cooked through.
- Mix the cooked eggs with the vegetables in the pan.
- Add soy sauce, sesame oil, salt, black pepper powder, white vinegar (if using), and red chili sauce or Sriracha (if using) to the pan. Stir well to combine.
- Add the cooked rice to the pan and toss everything together until the rice is evenly coated with the sauce and heated through.
- Taste the fried rice and adjust the seasoning if necessary.
- Garnish with chopped green onions and fresh coriander leaves if desired.
- Serve hot and enjoy your delicious Vegetable Fried Rice!

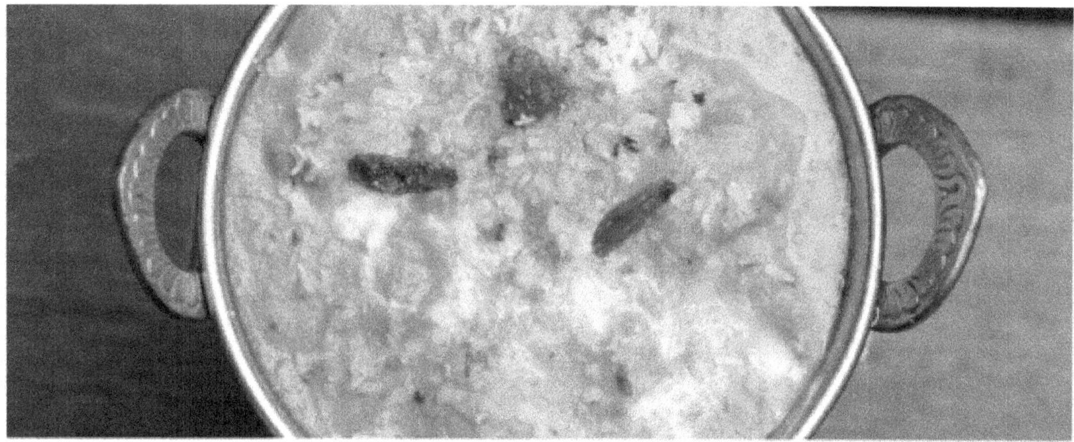

Dum Aloo

SERVINGS: 4   **PREPPING TIME: 15 MIN**   **COOKING TIME: 30 MIN**

Ingredients

- Baby potatoes: 500 grams
- Oil: for deep frying
- Yogurt: 1 cup
- Onion: 1 large, finely chopped
- Tomato: 1 large, finely chopped
- Ginger-garlic paste: 1 tablespoon
- Green chilies: 2, slit
- Cashew nuts: 10-12, soaked in water for 30 minutes
- Bay leaf: 1
- Cumin seeds: 1 teaspoon
- Turmeric powder: 1/2 teaspoon
- Red chili powder: 1 teaspoon
- Coriander powder: 1 teaspoon
- Garam masala: 1/2 teaspoon
- Salt: to taste
- Fresh coriander leaves: for garnish

Directions

Preparing the Potatoes:

- Wash and scrub the baby potatoes thoroughly to remove dirt.
- Parboil the potatoes in salted water for 8-10 minutes until they are slightly tender. Drain and let them cool.
- Once cooled, prick the potatoes with a fork or toothpick to ensure they absorb the flavors of the curry.
- Heat oil in a deep frying pan. Fry the potatoes until they turn golden brown and crispy. Drain them on paper towels to remove excess oil. Set aside.

Making the Gravy:

- In a blender, grind the soaked cashew nuts into a smooth paste.
- Heat 2 tablespoons of oil in a pan. Add bay leaf and cumin seeds. Let them splutter.
- Add chopped onions and sauté until they turn golden brown.
- Add ginger-garlic paste and slit green chilies. Sauté for a minute.
- Add chopped tomatoes and cook until they turn soft and mushy.
- Add turmeric powder, red chili powder, coriander powder, garam masala, and salt. Mix well and cook for 2-3 minutes.
- Add beaten yogurt and cashew nut paste. Stir continuously until the gravy thickens and the oil separates from the sides of the pan.
- Add the fried potatoes to the gravy. Mix gently to coat the potatoes with the gravy.
- Cover the pan with a lid and let the potatoes simmer in the gravy on low heat for 10-12 minutes. This will allow the potatoes to absorb the flavors of the gravy.

Garnish and serve the Dum Aloo with freshly chopped coriander leaves along with Butter Naan, Roti, or Stemed Rice.

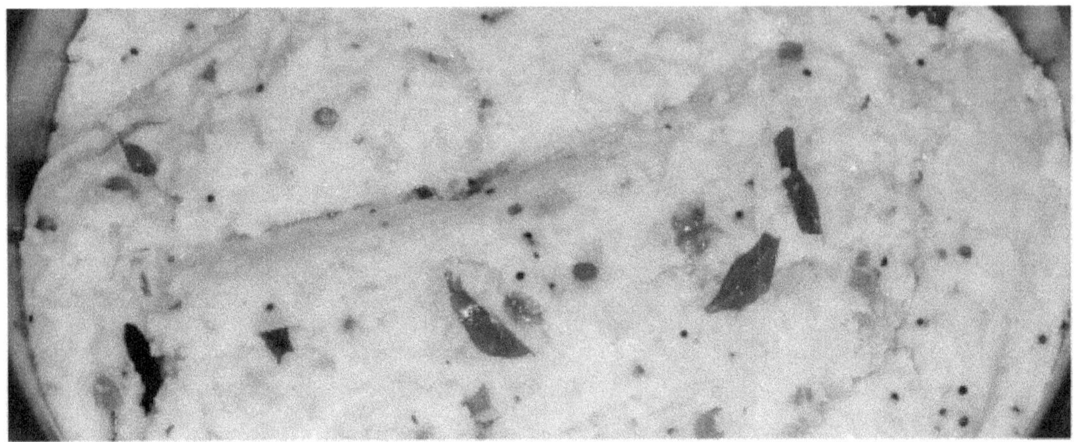

Suji (Rava) Upma

SERVINGS: 4　　　**PREPPING TIME: 15 MIN**　　　**COOKING TIME: 30 MIN**

Ingredients

- Rava (semolina): 1 cup
- Water: 2 cups, Oil: 2 tablespoons
- Mustard seeds: 1 teaspoon
- Urad dal (split black gram): 1 teaspoon
- Chana dal (split chickpeas): 1 teaspoon
- Curry leaves: Green chilies: 2, chopped
- Ginger: 1-inch piece, finely chopped
- Onion: 1 medium, finely chopped
- Carrot: 1 small, finely chopped (optional)
- Green peas: 1/4 cup (optional)
- Salt: to taste
- Fresh coriander leaves: for garnish (optional) Lemon juice: 1 tablespoon (optional)
-

Directions

Roasting the Rava

- Heat a dry skillet or pan over medium heat. Add the rava and roast it for 5-7 minutes, stirring constantly, until it turns light golden brown and fragrant. Be careful not to burn it. Transfer the roasted rava to a plate and set aside.

Making the Upma:

- In the same pan, heat oil over medium heat. Add mustard seeds and let them splutter.
- Add urad dal and chana dal. Sauté until they turn golden brown.
- Add curry leaves, chopped green chilies, and chopped ginger. Sauté for a minute until aromatic.
- Add chopped onions and sauté until they turn translucent.
- If using, add chopped carrots and green peas. Sauté for a couple of minutes until the vegetables are slightly tender.
- Pour 2 cups of water into the pan. Add salt to taste. Bring the water to a boil.
- Reduce the heat to low. Slowly add the roasted rava to the boiling water while stirring continuously to prevent lumps from forming.
- Cook the Upma on low heat for 5-7 minutes, stirring occasionally, until the rava absorbs all the water and becomes soft and fluffy.
- If desired, squeeze in some lemon juice garnish with fresh coriander leaves, and serve Hot. Ideal for Dinner !!!!

Fish Curry with Rice

<u>**SERVINGS: 4**</u>   **PREPPING TIME: 15 MIN**   **COOKING TIME: 30 MIN**

Ingredients

- Fish fillets
- Onion
- Tomato
- Ginger-garlic paste
- Fish curry spices (cumin, coriander, turmeric, chili powder)
- Coconut milk
- Curry leaves
- Oil
- Salt

Directions

- Wash the fish thoroughly under cold running water to remove any impurities.
- Pat the fish dry with paper towels and cut it into desired-sized pieces. Season the fish pieces with a pinch of salt and turmeric powder. Set aside.
- Sauté onions, tomatoes, and ginger-garlic paste until soft.
- Add fish curry spices and cook until fragrant.
- Add fish fillets and cook until tender.
- Pour in coconut milk, add curry leaves, and simmer until flavors meld.
- Serve hot with rice or appam.
- Taste: Tangy and spicy curry with tender fish fillets, creamy and flavorful with a hint of coconut milk.
- Sere it with steamed Rice.

Dal Fry

SERVINGS: 4   **PREPPING TIME: 10 MIN**   **COOKING TIME: 20 MIN**

Ingredients

- Toor dal (pigeon pea lentils): 1 cup
- Water: 3 cups, Oil or ghee: 2 tbs
- Cumin seeds: 1 tbs,
- Garlic: 4-5 cloves, Ginger: 1-inch
- Green chilies: 2, slit
- Onion: 1, Tomato: 1, finely chopped
- Turmeric powder: 1/2 teaspoon
- Red chili powder: 1/2 teaspoon
- Coriander powder: 1 teaspoon
- Garam masala: 1/2 teaspoon
- Salt: to taste
- Fresh coriander leaves: for garnish

Directions

- Rinse the toor dal under cold running water until the water runs clear.
- In a pressure cooker or a large pot, add the rinsed toor dal and 3 cups of water.
- Pressure cook the dal for 3-4 whistles or cook it in a pot until it becomes soft and mushy. If using a pressure cooker, allow the pressure to release naturally before opening the lid.
- Once cooked, mash the dal with the back of a spoon or a potato masher until smooth. Set aside.

How to Prepare

- Heat oil or ghee in a pan over medium heat.
- Add cumin seeds and let them splutter.
- Add minced garlic, chopped ginger, and slit green chilies. Sauté for a minute until aromatic.
- Add finely chopped onions and sauté until they turn golden brown.
- Add chopped tomatoes and cook until they become soft and mushy.
- Add turmeric powder, red chili powder, coriander powder, and garam masala. Mix well and cook for 2-3 minutes until the spices are fragrant.
- Pour the cooked and mashed dal into the pan. Stir well to combine with the onion-tomato mixture.
- Add salt to taste and adjust the consistency of the dal.
- Let the dal simmer for 5-7 minutes to allow the flavors to meld.
- Garnish the dal fry with freshly chopped coriander leaves. and serve hot.

Glossary of Indian Ingredients and Terms:

Garam Masala: A blend of ground spices commonly used in Indian cooking, typically including cinnamon, cardamom, cloves, cumin, and coriander.

Turmeric: A bright yellow spice with a warm, earthy flavour, known for its anti-inflammatory properties.

Cumin: A pungent spice with a warm, slightly bitter flavour, commonly used in curries, soups, and rice dishes.

Coriander: Both the seeds and leaves of the coriander plant are used in Indian cooking, imparting a citrusy, floral flavour.

Fenugreek: Aromatic seeds with a slightly bitter taste, often used in spice blends and pickles.

Mustard Seeds: Small seeds with a pungent flavour, used for tempering and pickling in Indian cuisine.

Curry Leaves: Aromatic leaves used to flavour dishes, particularly in South Indian cooking.

Tamarind: A sour fruit used as a souring agent in Indian dishes, such as chutneys and curries.

Kasuri Methi: Dried fenugreek leaves used to add a unique flavour to dishes, especially in North Indian cuisine.

Asafoetida (Hing): A pungent spice used in small quantities to enhance the flavour of dishes, particularly in lentil and vegetable preparations.

Chili Powder: Ground dried chilies used to add heat and colour to dishes, available in various heat levels.

Green Chilies: Fresh, green chili peppers used to add heat and flavour to dishes, commonly used in Indian cooking.

Ghee: Clarified butter used as a cooking fat and flavouring agent in Indian cuisine, prized for its rich, nutty flavour.

Paneer: Fresh Indian cheese made by curdling milk and then straining the whey, used in various vegetarian dishes.

Basmati Rice: A fragrant, long-grain rice variety commonly used in Indian cooking, prized for its aromatic flavour and fluffy texture.

Chana Dal: Split chickpeas used in various lentil dishes and snacks, known for their nutty flavour and firm texture.

Urad Dal: Black lentils commonly used in South Indian cuisine, especially for making dosa and idli batter.

Moong Dal: Split mung beans used in soups, stews, and dal preparations, known for their quick cooking time and delicate flavour.

Jaggery: Unrefined cane sugar used as a sweetener in Indian desserts and beverages, known for its caramel-like flavour.

Coconut Milk: A creamy liquid extracted from grated coconut flesh, used as a base for curries, soups, and desserts.

Papad: Thin, crispy discs made from lentil or chickpea flour, often served as a crunchy accompaniment to meals.

Roti: Unleavened flatbread made from whole wheat flour, a staple in North Indian cuisine.

Naan: Soft, leavened bread typically cooked in a tandoor oven, popular in North Indian cuisine.

Sambar: A tangy and spicy lentil-based vegetable stew, commonly eaten with rice or idli in South India.

Raita: A yogurt-based side dish flavoured with herbs, spices, and vegetables, served as a cooling accompaniment to spicy dishes.

Aloo: Potatoes, commonly used in various Indian dishes such as curries, parathas, and snacks.

Matar: Green peas, used in curries, rice dishes, and snacks.

Bhindi: Okra or ladyfinger, often used in stir-fries, curries, and pakoras.

Baingan: Eggplant or aubergine, used in curries, stir-fries, and stuffed dishes.

Kofta: Deep-fried or baked dumplings made from minced vegetables, paneer, or meat, served in rich, creamy gravies.

Masoor Dal: Red lentils used in various dal preparations, soups, and stews, known for their quick cooking time and earthy flavour.

Chaat: A Savory snack or street food made with a combination of fried dough, potatoes, chickpeas, yogurt, and tangy chutneys.

Pani Puri: Bite-sized hollow puris filled with a spicy, tangy water, potatoes, chickpeas, and tamarind chutney, a popular street food.

Chutney: A condiment made from a combination of fruits, vegetables, herbs, and spices, often served as a accompaniment to meals.

Lassi: A traditional Indian drink made from yogurt, water, and spices, sweetened or salted, served chilled.

Rasam: A tangy and spicy South Indian soup made with tamarind, tomatoes, and spices, often eaten with rice.

Dhokla: A Savory steamed cake made from fermented batter of rice and chickpea flour, a popular snack from Gujarat.

Samosa: A deep-fried pastry filled with spiced potatoes, peas, and sometimes minced meat, a popular snack in India.

Pav Bhaji: A spicy mashed vegetable curry served with buttered bread rolls, a popular street food from Mumbai.

Rasgulla: Soft and spongy cheese balls soaked in sugar syrup, a popular Bengali dessert.

Hope this glossary provides an overview of common Indian ingredients and terms used in traditional Indian cooking, offering insight into the rich and diverse culinary heritage of the country. Happy Reading and Happy Cooking!!!

I am sure you are going to try all of the dishes one after another. Do send me a picture of the dish made by you to prabhakar.veeraraghavan@gmail.com as I love to see pictures of dishes.

Closing Notes

Dear Readers,

As we come to the end of our culinary journey through the Flavors of India, I hope you have savoured every moment and every dish along the way. From exploring the rich tapestry of Indian culture to sharing delightful culinary stories and anecdotes, we've embarked on a flavourful odyssey that has surely left its mark on our hearts and palates.

Throughout this book, we've delved into the diverse cuisines of India, from the spicy delights of North India to the aromatic Flavors of South India, and everything in between. We've learned about the customs, traditions, and lifestyles that shape Indian cooking, and we've experienced the joy of creating delicious dishes in our own kitchens.

As you close this book, I hope you feel inspired and empowered to continue your culinary adventures. Whether you're craving the comfort of a warm bowl of dal or the excitement of trying your hand at homemade dosas, there's always something new to discover and enjoy.

Thank you for joining me on this journey, and I hope to see you again soon as we explore the Flavors of other cuisines from around the world. Until then, happy cooking and bon appétit!

If you found this book valuable, I kindly encourage you to share your feedback by leaving a positive review on platforms like Amazon or other media as your support can assist countless other Food lovers across the Universe.

With warm regards,

Prabhakar

Don't forget to explore more on my website! Scan the QR code below or visit <u>https://**prabhakarbookshelf.in**</u>[1] to discover a world of captivating stories waiting for you. Whether you're craving more adventures, mysteries, or heartfelt tales, there's something for every reader on Prabhakar Bookshelf.

And while you're there, don't miss out on the **<u>Freebies section</u>** where you can claim your free eBooks as a token of appreciation for your support. I believe in the joy of sharing knowledge and enriching lives. That's why I have dedicated a special page just for you in this **<u>Freebies section</u>**. I want every visitor to leave my website with something valuable, whether it's a free e-book, an insightful guide, or exclusive content. Happy reading!

Page |

Don't miss out!

Visit the website below and you can sign up to receive emails whenever Prabhakar Veeraraghavan publishes a new book. There's no charge and no obligation.

https://books2read.com/r/B-A-TUBX-OLEYC

BOOKS 2 READ

Connecting independent readers to independent writers.